ITALIAN
HOME COOKING

ITALIAN
HOME COOKING

125 RECIPES TO COMFORT YOUR SOUL

JULIA DELLA CROCE

PHOTOGRAPHS BY CHRISTOPHER HIRSHEIMER

KYLE BOOKS

For my father, born Giovanni Giuseppe della Croce,
April 13, 1908, Torito, Puglia, Italy; died John Dellacroce,
February 1, 2008, Suffern, New York, U.S.A.

Published in 2010 by Kyle Books,
an imprint of Kyle Cathie Ltd.
www.kylebooks.com

Distributed by National Book Network
4501 Forbes Blvd., Suite 200
Lanham, MD 20706
Phone: (800) 462-6420 Fax: (301) 429-5746
custserv@nbnbooks.com

978-1-906868-27-7

Text © 2010 Julia della Croce
Food photography © 2010 Christopher Hirsheimer
Location photography © 2010 Paolo Destefanis
Book design © 2010 Kyle Cathie Limited

Project editor Anja Schmidt
Designer Sara Schneider
Photographer Christopher Hirsheimer
Styling Melissa Hamilton
Copyeditor Janet McDonald
Production Lisa Pinnell and Gemma Jordan

Library of Congress Control Number: 2010933239

Color reproduction by Sang Choy
Printed and bound in China by C & C Offset Printing Co.

Contents

INTRODUCTION

"In Italy, food is considered to be good only in homes where there is an old lady wearing slippers in the kitchen."

— Francesco Antonucci, chef and restaurateur, Remi, 2005

In the summer of 1967, I made my first trip to Italy to meet family I'd never known. I immediately felt that I'd come home. The sea of Sardinia, the light, the colors, all cast a spell over me and the people captured my heart. And then there was the food! Newly discovered relatives overwhelmed my senses with local dishes: Zia Anna preparing a rabbit and olive stew; Zia Nella a capon with bread, sausage, and saffron stuffing; cousin Ida a suckling pig roasted on a bed of myrtle leaves. On Sundays, we piled into boats on the Cagliari Bay and plucked sea urchins from their pink coral beds, anointing our catch with juice from the fat lemons we'd picked along the coastal road. The food was better than anything I'd eaten before.

Since then, whether living abroad or in America, I have been drawn to the delights and comforts of Italian food. I have been nourished by it and, in turn, have nourished others with it. There is nothing about it that I do not love. Even the rituals of preparation and the rhythms of the harvest season bring comfort and anticipation, like the swish of the mezzaluna blade mincing the *battuto* on a wooden cutting board for Sunday ragù, or the robust cadence of the market as men set up their produce stalls early in the morning. But what I would not have imagined half a century ago has become a reality: home cooking is disappearing now that so many women, the customary standard bearers of culinary traditions, are in the work force.

Historically, Italian cooking has been a feminine art—an expression of creativity and imagination even when resources were scarce. With the food supply close at hand—in the garden or foraged from the countryside, from the hunter's catch or the fisherman's haul—women created a cuisine that has lasted millennia and captured more souls than the Roman Empire—without bloodshed.

Who will be the guardians of cooking traditions now? Much *alta cucina* is so astonishing in its technical achievement and aesthetic sophistication that its flavor seems almost secondary. Today, most culinary school graduates want to invent contemporary gastronomy, not reproduce the cooking of their grandmothers.

The rapid technological changes of modern life make it even more important for us to remember the exquisite sense of well-being, the warmth and excitement we once derived from eating food slowly and lovingly cooked at home. This book is an homage to that kind of food; to the kitchens of the Italian people, my own family of devoted cooks included, who have developed and preserved Italian cooking through the centuries and—during waves of immigration—across oceans to new worlds.

Those fortunate enough to have eaten in an Italian home where an "old lady wearing slippers" still possesses the knowledge of these food traditions will understand what others have missed. In America, we call it "comfort food." The Italians call it *cucina casalinga*, "home cuisine," and it is a highly evolved art form. It is the Italian food I love best, and you will find it in these pages.

AUTHOR'S NOTE TO THIS VOLUME:

The question inevitably arises about what dishes are traditional and what dishes are not. Because cuisine is a living craft based on products of the earth, it is always changing. The availability of foods, modern agricultural practices, dietary trends, foreign and cultural influences, and our current environmental responsibilities are just a few of the evolutionary factors in play. But whether recipes are part of a family's heritage or are newly created, there remains an essential difference between home cooking—comfort food—and professional cooking. *Cucina casalinga* is casual and relaxed, designed to sustain the body and uplift the spirit. Readers will find that this collection of recipes reflects the rustic, simple elegance of the best in Italian home cooking.

1

WELCOMING DISHES:
APPETIZERS, SAVORIES, AND SNACKS

Italians are nurturing and hospitable, especially at the table. Of welcoming dishes there is no end, and almost no end to their names, too. Called *spuntini* (from the verb meaning "spring up," suggesting spontaneity) or *intermezzi* ("interludes"), and most often *antipasti* (literally, "before the meal"), they are appetizers at meals or snacks in between. Italians love to *pizzicare* (to "pick at") many dishes on the table, sampling instead of overindulging. Several *antipasti* can combine as a light meal on their own. If pasta is served at lunch, dinner is often light, served with side dishes such as the ones I've included in this chapter. *Antipasti* are informal pleasures—creative but casual in their many forms: *salumi* (prosciutto, speck, mortadella, coppa, salami, and other cold cuts), vegetable compotes, breads and pies, *bruschette* and *crostini,* salads (see Chapter 3), and fritters beyond counting. I confess that I love them all, and some of my favorites are offered here.

CREAMY EGGPLANT SPREAD
ON BRUSCHETTA

Serves 4

The Italians have so many delicious ways of cooking eggplant, but this, perhaps one of the simplest, is a favorite of my daughter, a vegetarian. The clear flavors of fresh eggplant and good olive oil pop because no herbs or spices distract save a pinch of oregano. The trick to transforming eggplant from bitter to sweet without salting it is to remove excess seeds after roasting or grilling (if charred on a wood-fired grill, the pulp will take on a pleasant smoky flavor).

2 MEDIUM ITALIAN EGGPLANTS

4 CLOVES GARLIC, UNPEELED

2 TEASPOONS WHITE WINE VINEGAR

6 TABLESPOONS EXTRA-VIRGIN OLIVE OIL

½ TEASPOON SEA SALT

FRESHLY GROUND BLACK PEPPER

FRESHLY SLICED AND TOASTED ARTISAN BREAD, FOR SERVING

¼ TEASPOON DRIED OREGANO, CRUSHED

1. Preheat an oven to 400°F.

2. Place the whole eggplants and garlic cloves on a baking sheet and slide the pan onto the middle rack of the oven. Roast the garlic until soft, about 15 minutes; remove from the oven and set aside. Roast the eggplant until completely soft and collapsed and the skin is blackened, about 40 minutes. Remove from the oven and allow to cool. Use a spoon to scoop and discard excess seeds from the eggplant. Put the pulp in a sieve and allow it to drain to release excess moisture, from 1 hour to overnight, chilled.

3. Peel and mash the garlic and place it and the eggplant pulp in the bowl of an electric mixer. Alternatively, place it in a mixing bowl and use a hand whisk. Add the vinegar. Using the whisk attachment, or whisking by hand, whisk the mixture while pouring in the olive oil little by little, as though you were making mayonnaise, until the eggplant mixture is creamy and light. Season with salt and pepper.

4. Spread the eggplant cream onto the warm toasted bread slices. Sprinkle with oregano and serve.

AHEAD-OF-TIME NOTE: This spread can be made well ahead of time and stored in a covered vessel, chilled, for up to 5 days.

BATTER-FRIED
SAGE LEAVES AND ZUCCHINI BLOSSOMS
Serves 4

My family looks forward to summer every year when we can make these beautiful little treats from the zucchini blossoms and sage out of our garden (once fried, sage loses its pungency but not its flavor). They are so easy to make and nearly foolproof if you use the right ingredients. You can serve them for snacks, as appetizers, or as a side dish with dinner; guests invariably love them. The combination of zucchini blossoms and sage is a happy union, but you can make either one separately. When zucchini blossoms aren't available, it is easy enough to find fresh sage year-round in the herb section of the supermarket.

PURE (NOT EXTRA VIRGIN) OLIVE, GRAPE-SEED, OR OTHER VEGETABLE OIL WITH A HIGH SMOKING POINT, FOR FRYING

½ CUP UNBLEACHED ALL-PURPOSE FLOUR

12 TABLESPOONS SPARKLING MINERAL WATER OR SELTZER WATER

12 ZUCCHINI BLOSSOMS WITH ABOUT 2 INCHES OF STEM LEFT INTACT

16 LARGE SAGE LEAVES WITH ABOUT 1 INCH OF STEM LEFT INTACT

SEA SALT

1. Fill a deep skillet or frying pan with enough oil to reach about 1 inch up the sides. Warm over medium heat until the oil is hot enough to make a sage leaf sizzle when dropped in.

2. In the meantime, put the flour into a mixing bowl large enough to accommodate a blossom. Pour in the sparkling water and mix with a whisk until the mixture is blended and smooth. It should have the consistency of beaten egg and easily coat a spoon. If the mixture is too thick, thin with a little more of the water.

3. Begin with the zucchini flowers. Wash the blossoms rapidly under cold running water and dry them gently on paper towels; check inside the flowers for insects; remove the stamens. Dip each of the blossoms into the batter just before you are ready to cook them, using the stem as a handle for slipping them into the pan. Put only as many blossoms or leaves into the oil as can fit without crowding. Fry until golden, about 3 minutes altogether, turning them over midway during cooking. Use a skimmer to retrieve them when they are done. Transfer to paper towels, taking care not to spread the flowers to avoid crushing them. Sprinkle them with salt immediately to ensure it will stick and keep them crisp. Follow the same procedure for frying and salting the sage leaves, only frying them about 1 minute. Serve at once.

STUFFED
SQUASH BLOSSOMS
Serves 4

I grow plentiful zucchini in my garden to ensure that there will be enough blossoms to satisfy my craving for them. This is one of my favorite ways of preparing them, learned as a girl by watching my aunt make them after our forays to the open-air markets near her apartment in Rome. Select flowers that are about 3 inches from the base of the blossom to their tips.

PURE OLIVE OIL, FOR FRYING

½ CUP UNBLEACHED ALL-PURPOSE FLOUR

12 TABLESPOONS SPARKLING MINERAL WATER OR SELTZER WATER

16 LARGE ZUCCHINI BLOSSOMS WITH ABOUT 2 INCHES OF STEM LEFT INTACT

¼ POUND FRESH MOZZARELLA, GENUINE CACIOCAVALLO, OR GENUINE ASIAGO FRESCO, CUT INTO 16 DICE

SEA SALT

1. Fill a deep skillet or frying pan with enough oil to reach about 1½ inches up the sides. Warm the oil over medium heat until it is sizzling hot.

2. Meanwhile, put the flour into a mixing bowl large enough for a blossom to fit. Pour in the sparkling water and mix with a whisk until the mixture is blended and smooth. It should have the consistency of beaten egg and easily coat a spoon. If the mixture is too thick, thin with a little more of the water.

3. Wash the blossoms rapidly under cold running water and dry them gently on paper towels; check inside the flowers for insects; remove the stamens. Slip a piece of cheese into each, then fold the flower closed, pressing gently to make the petals adhere to each other.

4. Just before you are ready to cook them, dip each of the blossoms into the batter, using the stem as a handle for slipping them into the pan. Put only as many blossoms into the oil as can fit without crowding. Fry until golden, about 5 minutes in all, turning them over midway during cooking. Use a skimmer to retrieve them when they are done. Transfer to paper towels, taking care to avoid crushing them. Sprinkle with salt immediately to ensure it will stick and keep the blossoms crisp. Serve at once.

OLIVE
PESTO
Serves 4

Few things are more evocative of childhood in an Italian home than olives, particularly luscious black olives from the southern regions. In our home, they studded pumpkin stew, pasta sauces, chicken casseroles, thick *baccalà* chowder, and countless other dishes. One can rely on olives to enliven just about anything, but they can also stand alone, such as in the pesto I devised for a tasty topping for anything from crackers or crusty bread to pasta or grilled fish. If you keep brine-cured pitted olives in your pantry, it takes only minutes to make. For a more elaborate version, you can add three anchovies, the zest of one lemon, a small minced red onion, and a couple of tablespoons of minced fresh parsley.

1 PINT PITTED BRINE-CURED BLACK OLIVES SUCH AS GAETA, KALAMATA, OR NIÇOISE

2 TEASPOONS FINELY MINCED FRESH MARJORAM OR 1 TEASPOON DRIED MARJORAM

1 LARGE CLOVE GARLIC, FINELY GRATED

¼ CUP EXTRA-VIRGIN OLIVE OIL, PLUS ADDITIONAL, IF NEEDED

THINLY SLICED, FRESHLY TOASTED PLAIN ARTISAN BREAD, OR PLAIN SALTED CRACKERS, FOR SERVING

1. In the vessel of a food processor, combine the olives, marjoram, garlic, and olive oil. Pulse to grind 3 to 4 seconds. The resulting mixture should have some texture. Avoid over-pulsing, which will make the mixture too pasty and smooth. Transfer to a small but ample serving bowl and stir in more extra-virgin olive oil, if needed.

2. Spread the pesto onto the warm toasted bread slices and serve.

AHEAD-OF-TIME NOTE: This spread can be made well ahead of time and stored in a refrigerator for up to 3 weeks.

CLASSIC
SICILIAN CAPONATA
Serves 4

This stellar sweet-and-sour eggplant compote is a staple on the Sicilian table, as it was on ours, despite my mother's Sardinian origin. Caponata is typically served as an appetizer in Sicily, but we children ate it happily as an after-school snack or a pick-me-up at any time of day. Serve it on lettuce leaves or freshly toasted slices of bread.

1 POUND ITALIAN EGGPLANTS

SEA SALT

PURE OLIVE OIL, FOR DEEP FRYING

3 TABLESPOONS EXTRA-VIRGIN OLIVE OIL

1 LARGE ONION, CHOPPED

4 LARGE CLOVES GARLIC, SMASHED

5 CELERY STALKS, STRINGS REMOVED, CUT INTO 1-INCH DICE

¼ CUP ITALIAN CAPERS PACKED IN SALT, RINSED THOROUGHLY

¼ CUP TART GREEN SICILIAN OLIVES, PITTED AND QUARTERED

1¼ CUPS CRUSHED TOMATOES, OR TOMATO SAUCE

1 TABLESPOON RED WINE VINEGAR, OR MORE TO TASTE

1 TABLESPOON SUGAR

FRESHLY GROUND BLACK PEPPER TO TASTE

3 TABLESPOONS MINCED FRESH BASIL

LETTUCE LEAVES OR TOASTED BREAD SLICES, FOR SERVING

1. Wash the eggplants and remove the stem and navel. Leave the skin on. Cut into 1-inch cubes and transfer to a colander. Sprinkle lightly with salt and place a dish with a weight on top. Place the colander in a clean sink or on a plate where it can drain unhampered for at least 1 hour to give the seeds time to release their bitter liquid. Pat the eggplant well with paper towels to blot moisture and salt.

2. Pour enough olive oil to reach 1 inch up the sides of a frying pan. When it is sizzling hot, add the eggplant and fry until colored and soft, about 5 minutes. Drain on paper towels and sprinkle immediately with sea salt; set aside.

3. In a skillet, warm the 3 tablespoons olive oil. Add the onion and garlic and sauté over medium heat until wilted, about 5 minutes. Add the celery and sauté until colored but still crisp, about 5 minutes. Add the eggplant, capers, and olives and toss. Stir in the tomatoes or tomato sauce, vinegar, sugar, pepper, and basil. Cook over low heat for 10 minutes. Cover and chill overnight to develop the flavors.

4. Check for seasoning before serving. Caponata is best eaten at room temperature. Serve on lettuce leaves or toasted bread.

AHEAD-OF-TIME NOTE: Caponata will keep for 1 week, chilled.

BAKED CLAMS
WITH BACON

Serves 4

Few dishes are more emblematic of the Italian-American family-style restaurant than baked clams. Italian clams are about the size of a man's thumbnail, so it is not surprising that this dish is never presented in Italy. Only the larger Eastern Littleneck clams are suitable for stuffing. The clams should not be larger than a silver dollar or they will be too tough.

24 LIVE LITTLENECK CLAMS

⅓ CUP SEA SALT OR KOSHER SALT

1 CUP CORNMEAL

FOR THE TOPPING

2 TABLESPOONS EXTRA-VIRGIN OLIVE OIL

1 LARGE CLOVE GARLIC, FINELY CHOPPED OR PASSED THROUGH A GARLIC PRESS

2 TABLESPOONS FINE DRIED BREAD CRUMBS

2 TABLESPOONS CHOPPED FRESH ROASTED OR BOTTLED ROASTED SWEET RED PEPPER

2 TEASPOONS CHOPPED FRESH FLAT-LEAF PARSLEY

¼ CUP FINELY CHOPPED PANCETTA OR BACON

DRY WHITE WINE, FOR SPRINKLING

2 LEMONS, CUT INTO WEDGES

1. Soak the clams for 3 to 4 hours in 1 gallon of water mixed with the sea salt and cornmeal. (Use sea salt or kosher salt, as the iodine in regular salt will kill them.) One hour before cooking, scrub and rinse the clams well with a stiff vegetable brush under cold running water until they are free of sand. Tap any open clams. If they close, keep them; if not, discard at once. Place the clams in a bowl of hot water for 10 minutes to facilitate opening. Meanwhile, preheat a broiler.

2. In a mixing bowl combine all the ingredients for the topping and mix well. Working over a bowl to catch any clam juice, insert a clam knife or a small, sturdy paring knife between a clam's shells and, with a horizontal movement, thrust the blade toward the muscle on the base of the shell to open it. Detach the flesh from the shell cavity to make it easier to lift out when eating. Leave the whole clam meat in one of its shells and discard the other shell. Repeat with the other clams.

3. Spoon an equal amount of the topping over each clam. Drizzle a little of the clam juice from the bowl over the topping, then sprinkle lightly with a little wine to keep the clams moist. Place the clams in a flameproof baking dish 9 inches from the broiler. Broil for 6 minutes, watching carefully so the topping does not burn. If it browns too quickly, move the rack farther from the flame and add a little more clam juice or wine before returning to the oven. Serve hot with lemon wedges.

CRISPY LITTLE
CALZONE
Makes 8 calzone

Yeast dough is delicious fried, and these homey calzone (literally, "big socks") shouldn't be overlooked in the repertoire of appetizers and snack food for children and adults alike (kids love them as much as they love pizza). Fillings can be as simple as anchovy fillets or slices of good *salame,* or a combination of ham or *salame* and mozzarella, which melt into a pleasing ooziness when the calzone are hot. You can bake them, if you prefer; see the note below.

1 RECIPE RAPHAEL ZOERI'S MILK DOUGH
FOR YEAST BREAD (PAGE 216)

SALAME, PROSCIUTTO, OR A GOOD
ITALIAN MELTING CHEESE SUCH AS
MOZZARELLA, CACIOCAVALLO, FONTINA,
OR STRACCHINO

OLIVE OIL OR VEGETABLE OIL, FOR FRYING

SEA SALT

1. Make the dough as directed; divide into pieces the size of a small peach. Stretch each piece out into a thin, 6-inch round.

2. Place a piece of salame, prosciutto, or cheese, or a combination of both, in the center and fold the disk in half. Moisten the edges with a little water and seal shut. Crimp the edges well to prevent the filling from leaking out.

3. Pour enough oil into a frying pan to reach about 1 inch up the sides. When it is hot enough to make the dough sizzle, slip the calzone into the pan and fry until golden brown on both sides (about 5 minutes in total). Don't skimp on the oil, because at least 1 inch is needed for the calzone to fry properly on both sides. Drain on paper towels. Sprinkle with sea salt while still very hot. Serve at once.

NOTE: To bake, preheat an oven to 400°F. Place the calzone on an oiled baking sheet and cook until golden, about 20 minutes.

RAPHAEL BOERI'S
PISSALADELLA
Makes 1

Here is a pizza-like flatbread much like one my paternal grandmother used to make as a treat for her eleven children. Even when times were lean, flour, yeast, and onions were not hard to come by. Her rustic version had origins in Puglia, where she was born, but there are many versions throughout Italy, such as this one, which I learned from Italian pastry chef Raphael Boeri. His yeast dough is enriched with milk and egg, which makes the pastry light and flaky. The onions cook very slowly in olive oil and water without caramelizing, which creates a very sweet, creamy, and nourishing topping. Please *don't* skimp on the anchovy paste here—it virtually melts into the olive oil and become indistinguishable on the topping except for the remarkable flavor it imparts. For a zestier version, scatter brine-cured black olives or whole anchovy fillets over the topping after baking.

1 RECIPE RAPHAEL BOERI'S MILK DOUGH FOR YEAST BREAD (PAGE 216)

EXTRA-VIRGIN OLIVE OIL, FOR OILING

FOR THE TOPPING

8 ONIONS, HALVED AND SLICED PAPER-THIN

½ CUP EXTRA-VIRGIN OLIVE OIL, LESS 2 TABLESPOONS RESERVED

½ CUP WATER

2 TABLESPOONS ANCHOVY PASTE

1 TEASPOON MINCED FRESH OREGANO, OR ½ TEASPOON DRIED CRUMBLED OREGANO

1 TEASPOON SEA SALT

FRESHLY GROUND BLACK PEPPER

2 LARGE VINE-RIPE TOMATOES, CUT INTO THIN SLICES

½ CUP PITTED AND SLICED GAETA, KALAMATA, OR NIÇOISE OLIVES, OR 12 ANCHOVY FILLETS (OPTIONAL)

1. Make the dough as directed on page 216. While it is rising, lightly oil a 12 x 17-inch sheet pan, or its equivalent; set aside.

2. Make the topping: combine the onions, olive oil, and water in an ample pot. Cover and cook over low heat until soft and creamy, 45 minutes, stirring frequently to prevent the onions from sticking to the bottom of the pan. Turn off the heat. Blend the 2 reserved tablespoons of olive oil with the anchovy paste and stir it into the onions, mixing thoroughly; season with the oregano, salt, and plenty of pepper.

3. Preheat an oven to 400°F. On a lightly floured work surface, use a rolling pin to roll out the dough as thin as you can, forming it into a rectangular shape that will fit the dimensions of the sheet pan; it should be no more than ¼ inch thick. Roll the dough up onto the rolling pin, lift it into place on the baking sheet, and unroll it into the pan. Go all around the pan, easing the dough in. Press out air pockets

with your fingertips and use a fork to prick holes all over the surface. Using a sharp knife or kitchen shears, trim off excess dough around the rim *after* leaving a 1-inch overhang all around. Use dough scraps for making a bun and bake it. (Note that while the *pissaladella* does not need to rise for a second time, the bun will need a second rise until double in size before baking.) Line the crust with a layer of sliced tomatoes.

4. Turn the still-hot onion topping out onto the tomatoes and use a rubber spatula to spread it evenly; allow it to rest for 5 minutes, then slide the *pissaladella* onto the middle rack of the oven. Bake until the edges are golden, 20 to 25 minutes. Take it out of the oven and arrange the olives or anchovy fillets on top, if using. Allow the pie to settle for 15 minutes. Use a pastry wheel or kitchen shears to cut it into tidy squares. Eat hot or warm.

NONNA GIULIA'S
LAMB AND ARTICHOKE EMPANADAS
Makes about 18

If you like meat pies, as I do, you'll love these empanadas, an heirloom recipe of my maternal grandmother and namesake, Giulia Esu. While they may sound more Spanish than Italian, empanadas are a legacy of Alghero, the ancient Spanish-built port on the island of Sardinia. The filling is the original, but the dough recipe (page 219), developed by my friend, food writer and pastry expert Susan Purdy, has evolved from a lard-based *millefoglie* into a richly flavored American-style pie-type crust. Pork or beef can be substituted with excellent results.

1 RECIPE NEW WORLD FLAKY PASTRY DOUGH (PAGE 219)

1¼ POUNDS LEAN BONELESS LAMB

2 TABLESPOONS EXTRA-VIRGIN OLIVE OIL

1 MEDIUM ONION, CHOPPED

2 LARGE CLOVES GARLIC, MINCED

1 CUP ROUGHLY CHOPPED COOKED FRESH OR FROZEN ARTICHOKE HEARTS

4 OUNCES STALE BREAD

½ CUP STOCK OR MILK, FOR SOAKING BREAD

4 TABLESPOONS CHOPPED FRESH FLAT-LEAF PARSLEY

⅓ CUP FRESHLY GRATED PECORINO, PARMIGIANO-REGGIANO, OR GRANA PADANO CHEESE

2 LARGE EGG YOLKS (RESERVE EGG WHITES)

¾ TEASPOON SALT

¼ TEASPOON FRESHLY GROUND BLACK OR WHITE PEPPER

1 TABLESPOON CHOPPED FRESH ROSEMARY, OR 1½ TEASPOONS DRIED ROSEMARY

FOR THE EGG WASH

1 WHOLE EGG BEATEN WITH 1 TEASPOON WATER

1. Make the pastry and chill.

2. To make the filling, dice the lamb and grind it in the bowl of a food processor fitted with a metal blade.

3. In a skillet, warm the oil. Add the onion, garlic, and artichokes and sauté over medium heat until the onion is wilted, 3 to 4 minutes. Add the meat and sauté gently until lightly browned on the surface and bright pink inside, about 2 minutes. Transfer the mixture to a medium bowl.

4. Trim the crusts off the bread. Place it in a bowl and pour in enough stock or milk to cover. Soak until softened. Squeeze the bread dry and crumble it; discard the stock or milk.

5. Add the crumbled bread, parsley, grated cheese, egg yolks, salt, pepper, and rosemary to the meat mixture. Mix well.

6. Preheat an oven to 375°F. Line 2 baking sheets with parchment paper. On a floured work surface, roll out the dough until just less than ¼ inch thick. Using a 3-inch cookie cutter, stamp out as many rounds as possible from the dough. Transfer to the prepared baking sheets. Gather the scraps together; roll out again and stamp out additional disks. Brush the rounds with the reserved egg whites.

7. Place a generous tablespoon of the filling in the center of each dough disk. Fold the dough over the filling to create a half-moon shaped empanada, lining up the edges. Use a fork to firmly crimp the edges. Use extra dough to make decorations. Brush the surface with the egg wash. Bake until golden, about 30 minutes. Serve warm.

PANINI
WITH FRESH MOZZARELLA, TOMATO, AND PESTO

Makes 4

A *panino* (*panini,* plural) is a sandwich. I originally created this sensational one for school-children. Despite their unfamiliarity with some of the ingredients (the pesto and the artisan bread), it became one of their favorite meals. For the sandwich shell, I use Roman pizza-by-the-yard, also called "pizza bianca," that is typical of Roman bakeries. Outside of the borders of Italy and New York City, where baker Jim Lahey, formerly of Sullivan Street Bakery fame, popularized this sensational bread, it is not yet well known. If you cannot find this superb thin, light, and flaky artisanal bread, substitute a good artisanal focaccia that can be sliced open horizontally to produce thin sandwich bread with a nice top and bottom crust. Alternatively, use *ciabatta.*

FLAT ARTISAN BREAD SUCH AS *PIZZA BIANCA,* FOCACCIA, OR *CIABATTA* FOR 4 PEOPLE

2 TABLESPOONS BASIL PESTO (PAGE 44)

1 LARGE FRESH, VINE-RIPENED TOMATO, CORED AND THINLY SLICED

SEA SALT, TO TASTE

½ POUND FRESHLY MADE MOZZARELLA, SLICED INTO 4 SLICES OF THE SAME SIZE

1. If using a flatbread, cut into 4 equal serving-size rectangles or squares. Then cut the bread in half horizontally to obtain a bottom and top. If using *ciabatta* or other artisan bread, slice a standard portion size from the loaf for each person, and slice it open like a book.

2. To assemble the sandwich, first smear a little pesto on the cut sides of both top and bottom bread slices. Lay a tomato slice over it and sprinkle with salt. Over that, lay the mozzarella slice. Put the lid on the sandwich and cut in half.

EGGPLANT
FRITTERS
Serves 4

A classic in the Italian fritter repertoire, these eggplant morsels are always a big hit whenever I serve them. They ooze comfort on a cold day.

PURE OLIVE OIL, FOR GREASING PAN AND FOR FRYING

1 MEDIUM EGGPLANT, ABOUT 1½ POUNDS

1 LARGE EGG

1 LARGE CLOVE GARLIC, MINCED

2 TABLESPOONS MINCED FRESH FLAT-LEAF PARSLEY

1 TEASPOON MINCED FRESH MARJORAM, OR ½ TEASPOON DRIED MARJORAM

SEA SALT, TO TASTE

FRESHLY GROUND BLACK PEPPER

¼ CUP BREAD CRUMBS, PLUS 1 CUP FOR DREDGING

1. Preheat an oven to 400°F.

2. Lightly oil a baking sheet with olive oil. Slice the eggplant in half lengthwise. Place each half cut side down on the pan. Roast until soft, about 30 minutes. Remove from the oven and allow to cool. Use a spoon to scoop excess seeds out of the eggplant; discard them. Scoop the flesh of the eggplant out of the skin and squeeze it to get rid of as much liquid as you can; mince and place in a colander to drain until you are ready to combine it with the other ingredients.

3. In a mixing bowl, beat the egg with the garlic, parsley, marjoram, 1 teaspoon salt, and pepper to taste. Add the minced eggplant and the ¼ cup bread crumbs. Thoroughly mix all the ingredients together. Chill for 1 hour or overnight.

4. Pour olive oil in a skillet to reach 1½ inches up the sides of the pan. Place over medium-high heat. Line a platter with paper towels. Spread the remaining bread crumbs on a plate. Remove the eggplant mixture from the refrigerator and, using your hands, form small balls the size of a walnut. When the oil is sizzling hot, roll the balls in the bread crumbs. Press to flatten into a cookie shape and slip them into the hot oil one at a time. Fry until crispy and golden, about 5 minutes in all, turning them over midway through cooking. Use a skimmer to transfer them to the paper towels. Sprinkle lightly with salt immediately. Cook all the fritters in this fashion. Serve hot.

ZUCCHINI
FRITTERS
Serves 4

At least half the weight of zucchini is water, which can make many zucchini dishes sodden. But these fritters are very light and delicate as a result of salting and draining the shredded raw zucchini prior to forming the batter. I can hardly get the tasty morsels from stove to table before little hands snatch them as quickly as they are fried.

2 POUNDS SMALL ZUCCHINI, EACH WEIGHING BETWEEN 6 AND 8 OUNCES

2 TEASPOONS SEA SALT, PLUS MORE FOR SPRINKLING

2 LARGE EGGS, BEATEN

3 TABLESPOONS FRESHLY GRATED AGED GENIUNE ASIAGO, PARMIGIANO-REGGIANO, OR GRANA PADANO

1 TABLESPOON ALL-PURPOSE UNBLEACHED WHITE FLOUR

1 TABLESPOON FINE BREAD CRUMBS

FRESHLY GROUND BLACK PEPPER

PURE OLIVE OIL, FOR FRYING

1. Wash the zucchini well and slice off the stem and navel. Grate them on the large holes of a box grater or with a shredding attachment in a food processor. Put the zucchini in a colander and sprinkle with 2 teaspoons salt. Place a plate on top. Over the plate, place a heavy weight such as a tea kettle filled with water or a very large can. Put the colander in the sink positioned over the drain. Allow the zucchini to release their water for at least an hour or up to two hours. Transfer the shredded zucchini to a clean kitchen towel to blot the remaining moisture, then place it in a mixing bowl, first using your hands to wring as much liquid out of the zucchini as possible.

2. Combine the shredded zucchini, eggs, cheese, flour, bread crumbs, and pepper. The mixture should be soft but not watery; if it is too thick, the fritters will be heavy. Chill the mixture for an hour or up to two hours.

3. Pour enough olive oil in a frying pan to come 1½ inches up the sides. Turn on the heat and when the oil is sizzling hot, slip the zucchini mixture in one rounded teaspoon at a time. Take care not to crowd the pan; the fritters need plenty of room to cook. Fry until golden and crisp, about 5 minutes in total, turning them over when they are golden brown on one side. Use a skimmer or tongs to transfer the fritters to paper towels to drain. Sprinkle with sea salt as soon as they are taken out of the oil and plenty hot. Repeat this procedure with the remaining batter. Serve the fritters at once.

SAVORY SUMMER SQUASH PANCAKES

Serves 4

Called *pizze fritte* in Calabria, these savory pancakes, which I learned from my neighbor's son, Chef Nick Gualano, are popular during the summer and autumn harvest when zucchini are profuse in the garden. They can be made with small zucchini (fewer seeds, less water content, and more flavor) or with zucchini blossoms. If using zucchini blossoms, first remove the stem and stamen, and slice the flower into ribbons; there is no need to salt and drain them first as for the squash. *Pizze fritte* are excellent for lunch or a light dinner, and they are best eaten hot as soon as they are made. To prepare zucchini blossoms, use the blossoms on the day you pick them or buy them. Wrap them loosely in damp paper towels and chill until ready to cook.

8 OUNCES ZUCCHINI OR YELLOW SUMMER SQUASH

2 TEASPOONS SEA SALT, PLUS MORE FOR SPRINKLING

2 LARGE EGGS

3 LARGE CLOVES GARLIC, MINCED

¼ TEASPOON FRESHLY GROUND BLACK PEPPER

½ CUP FRESHLY *GRATED* PARMIGIANO-REGGIANO, PECORINO ROMANO OR GRANA PADANO CHEESE

¼ CUP UNBLEACHED ALL-PURPOSE FLOUR

OLIVE OIL, FOR FRYING

1. Grate the squash on the coarse side of a box grater, or shred it using the shredding attachment of a food processor; transfer it to a colander. Toss with 1 teaspoon of the salt. Put the colander in a sink and place a plate and heavy weight such as a large, filled can on top. Allow the liquid to drain, about 30 minutes. Using your hands, squeeze as much liquid from the squash as you can.

2. Beat the eggs and add the garlic, the other teaspoon of salt, pepper, and grated cheese. Whisk in the flour. Fold in the squash.

3. Warm 3 tablespoons of the olive oil over medium heat in an ample frying pan. Drop 2 tablespoons of the squash batter in the pan to form small pancakes. Fry until golden on both sides, about 4 minutes. Transfer to a serving dish. Sprinkle salt on the pancakes as soon as they come out of the pan. Serve at once.

2

EVERYDAY SAUCES AND DRESSINGS

When I once asked a cousin how he'd found the food in France, he replied, "I don't know. There was so much sauce on everything I couldn't tell." The Italian way with sauces (and dressings) is different. For most meats and fish, the natural juices suffice when fortified with wine, vinegar, lemon, or herbs. Olive oil alone, before cooking or after, brings out the flavors of many simple dishes. Most important are the tomato and meat sauces for pasta and polenta, as in the Neapolitan saying, *Criste mì, fa chiove le maccarrune, e le chianghe de le logge fatta ragù;* "Sweet Jesus, make it rain macaroni, and turn our balconies into pots of ragù." One of the most comforting rituals of Sundays and holidays is the rite of their preparation, which begins early in the morning. Mother or grandmother is up long before the rest of the household, gently clanging her pots and pans, a clatter far kinder to the sleepy ear than any raucous alarm clock. To Italian cooks, sauces are like reflexes, even instincts, and there is no one standard or "best" recipe for any of them. Here are the ones I turn to time and time again.

FRUITY NEAPOLITAN TOMATO SAUCE
("POMAROLA")

Makes 2 cups

I learned to make *Pomarola,* or *ummarola* in dialect, a traditional sauce for spaghetti and macaroni, from my aunt, who lived in Naples for much of her life. It consists of fresh tomatoes in season, or canned tomatoes. Because it begins with a generous *battuto* (a vegetable base), it is fruity and fragrant and has a great deal of texture. It is well suited to the texture of dried pasta; linguine and bucatini are especially compatible with it, and this recipe is enough for a pound of it. When sieved, *pomarola* can be used as a foundation for other sauces or ragù.

2½ CUPS CANNED, PEELED PLUM TOMATOES IN JUICE, OR 2½ POUNDS FRESH, SWEET, MATURE VINE-RIPENED PLUM TOMATOES, PEELED, SEEDED, AND CHOPPED (SEE STEP 1)

4 TABLESPOONS EXTRA-VIRGIN OLIVE OIL

2 LARGE CLOVES GARLIC, CRUSHED

1 SMALL RED ONION, MINCED

1 MEDIUM CELERY STALK, INCLUDING LEAVES, MINCED

1 SMALL CARROT, MINCED

2 TABLESPOONS FRESH FLAT-LEAF PARSLEY, MINCED

SMALL HANDFUL OF CHOPPED FRESH BASIL

2 TABLESPOONS TOMATO PASTE

SCANT ½ TEASPOON SALT, OR TO TASTE

FRESHLY GROUND BLACK OR WHITE PEPPER

1. If using canned tomatoes, drain them and reserve their juice; chop and set aside. If using fresh tomatoes, bring a large saucepan three quarters full of water to a boil. Blanch the tomatoes for 30 to 45 seconds; drain and immediately plunge into cold water. Using a paring knife, lift off the skins and cut out the tough area around the core. Cut the tomatoes into quarters lengthwise, push out excess seeds, and chop.

2. In a saucepan over medium-low heat, warm 3 tablespoons of the olive oil. Stir in the garlic, onion, celery, carrot, parsley, and basil, and sauté until completely soft, about 12 minutes. Add the tomato paste and sauté for 3 minutes. Then add the tomatoes and their juice, cover partially, and simmer gently until thickened, about 45 minutes. Season to taste. Remove from the heat and stir in the remaining 1 tablespoon olive oil before serving.

NOTE: To make a smooth sauce, let cool and then pass through a food mill over a clean saucepan, pressing out as much pulp as possible. Place over medium heat just to heat through, about 3 minutes. Remove from the heat and stir in the remaining olive oil.

AHEAD-OF-TIME NOTE: The sauce can be made 4 to 5 days ahead of time and stored tightly covered in the refrigerator, or it can be frozen for up to 3 months. Leave out the remaining 1 tablespoon olive oil and stir it into the sauce after reheating.

LONG-SIMMERED
BOLOGNESE MEAT SAUCE

Makes 2 cups

Salsa bolognese, also known as *ragù bolognese,* has traveled far and wide outside the borders of Bologna, and no wonder. This complex, fragrant, and delicate meat sauce, versions of which simmer in pots all over the region of Emilia-Romagna in preparation for midday Sunday lunch, is one of the marvels of the Italian table. While I have listed ground beef in this recipe, a combination of veal, pork, and beef can be used for an even more complex sauce. *Salsa bolognese* is typically used between layers of homemade lasagne in Bologna's region, and it is the classic sauce for homemade tagliatelle. Pappardelle and fettuccine are also suitable matches. The most compatible macaroni cuts are fusilli corti (short twists), gnocchetti, and rigatoni. Pass freshly grated Parmigiano-Reggiano at the table.

2½ CUPS CANNED, PEELED PLUM TOMATOES IN JUICE

3 TABLESPOONS UNSALTED BUTTER

1 TABLESPOON EXTRA-VIRGIN OLIVE OIL

1 SMALL WHITE OR YELLOW ONION, FINELY CHOPPED

1 SMALL CELERY STALK, INCLUDING LEAVES, FINELY CHOPPED

½ SMALL CARROT, SCRAPED AND FINELY CHOPPED

1 TABLESPOON CHOPPED FRESH FLAT-LEAF PARSLEY

¾ POUND GROUND LEAN BEEF, PREFERABLY CHUCK

½ TEASPOON SALT, OR TO TASTE

½ CUP GOOD-QUALITY DRY WHITE WINE

⅔ CUP MILK

⅛ TEASPOON NUTMEG, PREFERABLY FRESHLY GRATED

FRESHLY GROUND WHITE OR BLACK PEPPER

TASTY MEAT BROTH, AS NEEDED (PAGE 213)

1 POUND PASTA, COOKED, FOR SERVING 4

1. Drain the tomatoes, reserving their juice. Chop and set aside.

2. In a large, wide Dutch oven or large, deep skillet over low heat, melt 2 tablespoons of the butter with the olive oil. Stir in the onion, celery, carrot, and parsley and sauté until quite soft but not at all browned, about 12 minutes. Keeping the heat very low, add the ground meat. The meat must heat very gently, only enough to color it lightly on the outside; preventing it from hardening allows it to absorb the flavors of the other ingredients and to become delicate and creamy. Stir in the salt and wine. Simmer very gently for several minutes until the the liquid is absorbed.

3. Add the milk and nutmeg. (It is important to add the milk before adding the tomatoes so that it is absorbed by the meat.) Simmer gently for 10 minutes, then add the tomatoes and juice. As soon as the sauce begins to simmer, turn the heat down as low as possible. Cover partially and simmer, always over the lowest heat

and stirring occasionally, for about 4 hours. If the sauce begins to dry out, stir in a little of the meat broth at a time. Check for seasoning. Serve over the cooked pasta.

AHEAD-OF-TIME NOTE: This sauce can be made 3 or 4 days in advance and stored tightly covered in the refrigerator or it can be frozen for up to 3 months. Leave out the remaining 1 tablespoon butter and the pepper. Stir them in after reheating the sauce.

20-MINUTE TOMATO SAUCE
WITH GARLIC

Makes 2 cups

This is a homey quick and chunky tomato sauce, rustic in character due to its texture and to the large quantity of garlic. I often use it for dried pasta dishes, or on freshly made gnocchi or ravioli.

2½ CUPS CANNED, PEELED PLUM TOMATOES IN JUICE	2 TABLESPOONS TOMATO PASTE
3 TABLESPOONS EXTRA-VIRGIN OLIVE OIL	2 OR 3 FRESH BASIL LEAVES
4 LARGE CLOVES GARLIC, SMASHED	¼ TEASPOON SALT, OR TO TASTE
	FRESHLY GROUND BLACK PEPPER

1. Drain the tomatoes, reserving their juice. Using your hands or a potato masher, crush the tomatoes well. Set aside.

2. In a cold saucepan over medium-low heat, warm 2 tablespoons of the olive oil and the garlic together, and sauté until the garlic is soft but not colored, 3 to 4 minutes. Add the tomato paste and stir; then add the tomatoes and their strained juice. Simmer over low heat, uncovered, until enough of the liquid evaporates to form a sauce that will coat a spoon, about 25 minutes. Tear the basil into small pieces and stir them into the sauce along with the salt. Simmer for another minute or two. Remove from the heat and stir in the pepper and the remaining 1 tablespoon olive oil.

VARIATION: Substitute 1 small red, white, or yellow onion, chopped, for the garlic.

AHEAD-OF-TIME NOTE: The sauce can be made 4 to 5 days in advance of using and stored tightly covered in the refrigerator, or it can be frozen for up to 3 months. Whether storing it in the refrigerator or freezer, leave out the basil, pepper, and last tablespoon olive oil. Stir them into the sauce after reheating.

ZIA RITA'S SARDINIAN
TOMATO SAUCE WITH BACON AND SAFFRON

Makes 2¾ cups

It is characteristic of Sardinian cooking to add saffron to sauces, as in this recipe, which I learned to make from my aunt, Rita Ghisu. Not only does saffron impart an incomparable and beguiling flavor, it gives the sauce a beautiful, deep golden cast. The back bacon enriches its flavor, but is removed after sautéing; the crispy lardoons are reserved for scattering on top before serving. This sauce is traditionally served with *malloreddus,* a pasta peculiar to the island. Cavatelli or conchiglie ("shells") are the closest substitutes. Pass freshly grated young (mild) Pecorino, Parmigiano-Reggiano, or Grana Padano at the table with the sauce.

2½ CUPS CANNED, PEELED PLUM TOMATOES IN JUICE

3 TABLESPOONS EXTRA-VIRGIN OLIVE OIL

2 OUNCES BACK BACON, THICK-SLICED AND CUT INTO MATCHSTICK STRIPS (LARDOONS)

4 LARGE CLOVES GARLIC, BRUISED

2 TABLESPOONS TOMATO PASTE

2 ENVELOPES (⅛ TEASPOON TOTAL) SAFFRON POWDER, OR ⅛ TEASPOON SAFFRON THREADS

SALT

4 FRESH BASIL LEAVES

1 POUND PASTA, COOKED, FOR SERVING 4

1. Drain the tomatoes, reserving their juice. Chop the tomatoes and set aside.

2. In a saucepan over low heat, warm the olive oil. Add the back bacon and sauté gently until it is colored nicely and crispy, about 2 minutes. Set aside. Increase the heat to medium-low, add the garlic, and sauté until lightly colored, about 8 minutes. Add the chopped tomatoes and their juice and simmer over medium-low heat until excess liquid from the tomatoes has evaporated, about 10 minutes. Stir in the tomato paste. If using saffron threads, dissolve them in a tablespoon of hot water and stir them into the sauce. If using saffron powder, simply stir it into the sauce. Season with salt and simmer gently, uncovered, over medium-low heat, until a thick consistency forms, about 30 minutes. Stir the sauce occasionally as it cooks.

3. Stir in the basil during the last 20 minutes of cooking. Taste and adjust the salt.

4. Toss with the hot pasta. Sprinkle each serving plate with some of the reserved crispy lardoons.

AHEAD-OF-TIME NOTE: This sauce can be made 4 or 5 days in advance and stored tightly covered in the refrigerator, or it can be frozen for up to 3 months. Leave out the basil until you reheat the sauce.

SOUTHERN-STYLE
BEEF AND PORK RAGÙ

Makes 2½ cups

Variations of this dense, richly flavored sauce are part of the landscape in kitchens all across the *Mezzogiorno,* as the southern regions of Italy are called. Making it is so much a part of local folklore that it has been the subject of vernacular poetry, song, and street theater. Its aroma is part of the fabric of my own childhood memories. This is how my mother made it. Use this sauce for spaghetti, or for macaroni cuts such as rigatoni, ziti, penne, or cavatelli.

3 CUPS CANNED, PEELED PLUM TOMATOES IN JUICE

1 POUND BEEF CHUCK STEAK, IN ONE PIECE

½ POUND PORK SHOULDER, IN ONE PIECE, OR 1 LARGE PORK CHOP WITH BONE

3 TABLESPOONS EXTRA-VIRGIN OLIVE OIL

2 LARGE CLOVES GARLIC, CRUSHED

1 MEDIUM RED ONION, MINCED

1 SMALL CARROT, SCRAPED AND MINCED

1 SMALL CELERY STALK, MINCED

½ CUP TOMATO PASTE

½ CUP GOOD-QUALITY DRY RED WINE

SALT AND FRESHLY GROUND BLACK PEPPER

¾ CUP WATER

1 TEASPOON CHOPPED FRESH BASIL

1 POUND PASTA, COOKED, FOR SERVING 4

1. Drain the tomatoes, reserving their juice. Chop and set aside. Trim excess fat from the steak and pork, but leave each of the meats in one piece.

2. In a heavy pot over medium-high heat, warm the olive oil and brown the meats on all sides, about 12 minutes. Transfer to a dish and set aside. Reduce the heat to medium-low, add the garlic, onion, carrot, and celery, and sauté until softened, about 10 minutes. Stir in the tomato paste and sauté for 3 minutes.

3. Return the meat with any juices to the pot and add the wine. Simmer, uncovered, until the liquid evaporates, about 3 minutes. Add the tomatoes and their juice and season with salt and pepper. Stir in the water and basil and bring to a boil. Reduce the heat to low, cover partially, and simmer, stirring occasionally, until the meat is tender and the sauce has thickened, about 1 hour and 45 minutes.

4. When the sauce is done, remove the meat and slice. Serve the sauce over pasta and the meat on a side dish. For a smooth sauce, cut the meat into dice and pass it together with the sauce through a food mill. A food processor will make a slightly thicker sauce, since it doesn't actually strain any part of it.

AHEAD-OF-TIME NOTE: This sauce can be made 3 or 4 days in advance and stored tightly covered in the refrigerator, or it can be frozen for up to 3 months.

MUSHROOM RAGÙ

Makes 2½ cups

Because my children were vegetarians throughout their childhoods, I created alternatives to the wonderful meat ragù that often bubbled on my stovetop and would seduce them. Here is one of the meatless sauces I created. The combination of dried porcini mushrooms and wild mushrooms give it astonishing flavor. As with all these sauce recipes, this is enough for one pound of pasta and can be paired with virtually all cuts that are appropriate for saucing. It can also be used as a side sauce with eggs or as a topping for polenta or simple rice dishes.

½ OUNCE DRIED PORCINI MUSHROOMS

8 OUNCES FRESH MUSHROOMS, INCLUDING SHIITAKE, OYSTER, OR CHANTERELLE

3 TABLESPOONS EXTRA-VIRGIN OLIVE OIL

2 TABLESPOONS UNSALTED BUTTER

4 LARGE CLOVES GARLIC, SLICED

1 SMALL ONION, CHOPPED

2 TEASPOONS MINCED FRESH ROSEMARY, OR 1 TABLESPOON DRIED CRUMBLED ROSEMARY

3 TABLESPOONS TOMATO PASTE

½ CUP GOOD-QUALITY DRY RED WINE

1 CUP TASTY MEAT BROTH (PAGE 213)

SALT AND FRESHLY GROUND BLACK PEPPER

1. Prepare the dried and fresh mushrooms: Soak the dried porcini in a small bowl with 1 cup hot water for 15 to 20 minutes. Use a slotted spoon to lift them out; rinse under running cold water to remove any sand or grit. Squeeze out the excess water and give them a rough chop. Strain the soaking liquid through cheesecloth or a paper towel-lined strainer to remove any grit. Set aside the mushrooms and the strained liquid separately. With a clean kitchen towel, wipe any dirt from the fresh mushrooms. Cut off any woody stem tips and slice them thin.

2. In a deep, nonstick skillet, combine the olive oil, butter, and garlic. Sauté gently until the garlic softens, about 1 minute. Stir in the onion and rosemary and sauté for another minute. Add the porcini and other mushrooms and sauté over medium heat until they sweat, about 5 minutes, tossing frequently.

3. Dilute the tomato paste in the reserved mushroom soaking liquid and add to the sauce. Stir in the wine. Simmer over medium-low heat until the liquid evaporates, about 1 minute. Pour in the broth and continue to simmer, until the flavors marry about 10 minutes. Season with salt and pepper.

AHEAD-OF-TIME NOTE: This sauce can be made 3 or 4 days in advance of using and stored tightly covered in the refrigerator, or it can be frozen for up to 3 months.

VIOLA BUITONI'S LONG-SIMMERED
TOMATO SAUCE with RIBS and SAUSAGES

Serves 4 to 6

In the early 1950s, Buitoni was a household word in my Italian family, transplanted in a new land where authentic ingredients were hard to come by. Many years later, I met Viola, the daughter of Buitoni pasta company founder Paolo Buitoni. She had an elite catering company in New York City and eventually opened her own Italian specialty food shop. This is one of her family recipes, a thick, succulent stew swimming with pork ribs and sweet sausage. Serve it with polenta (see page 217) or pasta.

5 TABLESPOONS EXTRA-VIRGIN OLIVE OIL

18 BABY BACK RIBS, OR 4 POUNDS "COUNTRY-STYLE" PORK RIBS (BONE-IN RIB ENDS), CUT OFF THE RACK INTO INDIVIDUAL RIBS

9 SWEET ITALIAN PORK SAUSAGES

1 ONION, MINCED

1 CARROT, MINCED

3 CELERY STALKS WITH LEAVES, MINCED

3 WHOLE ROSEMARY SPRIGS, LEAVES REMOVED AND MINCED, OR 1 TEASPOON CRUMBLED DRIED ROSEMARY

½ CUP DRY RED WINE

5 CUPS (56 OUNCES) CANNED ITALIAN PLUM TOMATOES, DRAINED (RESERVE JUICES), SEEDED, AND CHOPPED

SEA SALT

1. In a large, heavy-bottomed wide Dutch oven, warm the olive oil over medium heat. Add the ribs and sausages, separating the links if they are attached. Sauté over medium-low to medium heat until lightly browned all over, about 25 minutes. Transfer the meat to a side dish and add the onion, carrot, celery, and rosemary to the pan. Reduce the heat to medium-low; sauté, stirring occasionally, until the vegetables are well softened, about 10 minutes.

2. Return the ribs and sausages to the pan and toss all together. Pour in the wine and stir to distribute well. Cook to evaporate the liquid, about 3 minutes. Add the tomatoes and their juice, cover, and simmer, stirring occasionally, until the sauce is thick and the meat is so tender it actually falls off the bones, 2½ to 3 hours. Remove from the heat, taste for salt, and serve.

BLANCHED BASIL PESTO
(FOOD PROCESSOR METHOD)

Makes 1 cup

In summer there is always plenty of basil growing in my garden. My daughter forever tends it and prunes its sprigs, and delivers baskets of it for me to make one of her favorite sauces, *pesto alla genovese*. This recipe differs from others I've published in that the basil is blanched before grinding. While this is a departure from the classic method, blanching prevents the basil from turning brown and surprisingly doesn't interfere with its flavor or texture. Pesto needs a sturdy pasta to support it—fettuccine, nidi, spaghetti, bucatini, or linguine.

1 TABLESPOON KOSHER SALT

2 CUPS FRESH BASIL LEAVES, SOLIDLY PACKED 2 CLOVES GARLIC, CUT INTO PIECES

⅓ CUP LIGHTLY TOASTED PINE NUTS

GENEROUS ½ TEASPOON SALT

FRESHLY GROUND BLACK PEPPER

½ CUP EXTRA-VIRGIN OLIVE OIL

½ CUP FRESHLY GRATED PARMIGIANO-REGGIANO CHEESE

2 TABLESPOONS UNSALTED BUTTER, SOFTENED TO ROOM TEMPERATURE

1 POUND PASTA, COOKED, FOR SERVING 4

1. In a saucepan, bring 1 quart water to a boil and add the kosher salt and basil leaves. Press the basil with a skimmer to keep it submerged for 30 seconds. Drain immediately and shock it in an ice-water bath to stop the cooking. Squeeze the basil leaves with your hands to remove excess water. Coarsely chop.

2. Put the basil, garlic, pine nuts, salt, a few grinds of pepper, and the oil into the vessel of a food processor. Blend to a smooth puree, stopping the machine once or twice to scrape the sides of the container. Add the grated cheeses and butter, and blend for about 15 seconds. Scrape the sides again and blend for another few seconds. Do not overprocess, or your pesto will have very little texture.

3. When cooking your pasta, save some of the cooking water and stir 1 tablespoon of it with the pesto before combining it with steaming hot pasta; use another few tablespoons or so to moisten the pasta when you toss the pesto with it.

NOTE: For a pesto with better texture, leave the grated cheese and butter out and beat them in by hand when you have finished blending the other ingredients.

KEEPING PESTO: Pesto will keep in the refrigerator for several months after transferring to a sealed glass jar. Push a layer of plastic wrap on the surface of the pesto. This is far more effective than the traditional method of pouring olive oil on the surface. Leave out the salt, cheese, and butter and beat them in just before using.

FRESH
TOMATO VINAIGRETTE

Makes 1¼ cups

This appealing tomato-colored dressing is best to make when a luscious and sweet freshly picked garden tomato is at hand. Toss it with leafy salads or cooked vegetable salads.

1 SWEET, VINE-RIPENED TOMATO	SEA SALT AND FRESHLY GROUND BLACK OR WHITE PEPPER
1 LARGE SHALLOT, MINCED	
1 TEASPOON DIJON MUSTARD	¼ CUP GOOD-QUALITY WHITE WINE VINEGAR OR SHERRY VINEGAR
FINELY MINCED FRESH FLAT-LEAF PARSLEY	¾ CUP OLIVE OIL

1. Cut the tomato in half and push out the seeds. Squeeze out excess juices and chop.

2. Combine the shallot, mustard, parsley, salt and pepper to taste, and vinegar and allow to macerate for up to an hour, if you have the time.

3. Stir in the olive oil and tomato and puree in a food processor; pulse for a few seconds more. Taste for seasoning.

WINE, CAPER, AND SHALLOT DRESSING

Makes ¾ cup

An alternative to vinegary dressings that interfere with tasting your wine when eating salad, this dressing uses wine instead of vinegar. Use a red wine that you can drink with your meal.

1 LARGE SHALLOT, MINCED	2 TEASPOONS ANCHOVY PASTE
2 TABLESPOONS DIJON MUSTARD	2 TABLESPOONS CHOPPED CAPERS
2 TABLESPOONS FINELY MINCED FRESH FLAT-LEAF PARSLEY	¼ CUP GOOD-QUALITY FULL-BODIED DRY RED WINE
SEA SALT AND FRESHLY GROUND BLACK OR WHITE PEPPER	½ CUP OLIVE OIL

1. Combine the shallot, mustard, parsley, sea salt, pepper to taste, anchovy paste, capers, and wine and allow to macerate for up to an hour, if you have the time.

2. Stir in the olive oil. Taste and adjust the salt if necessary.

3

TO YOUR HEALTH:
LEAFY AND COMPOSED SALADS

The map shows why Italians love vegetables: All those mountains! So little farmland! (And even the steepest slopes have been laboriously terraced for a few extra acres to cultivate.) From childhood, vegetables have been treats to Italians. Green leaves, tomatoes, and a shower of shredded carrots, and perhaps some field greens, aid digestion and clear the palate; but they are more important for their link to the family and the land. There is variety in plenty: tender lettuces, bitter chicory, or bold radicchio for accents; beet greens for color and health; arugula for bite. Elaborate salads include asparagus or zucchini, rice, potatoes, grains, beans, eggs, meat, and seafood. (But never pasta. In Italy, pasta is served hot and eaten immediately. Don't wait for everyone to be served.) Salads are appetizers or side dishes; and they may replace hot meals in summer or join the mosaic of the antipasto table. Olive oil—seductive or assertive—and wine vinegar or lemon juice are musts for most dressings, although, for a few salads, nothing will do but fresh mayonnaise (see page 218). Here is an assortment of salads for an informal meal, the buffet table, or a portable feast.

RICE AND SHRIMP SALAD
WITH PINE NUTS

Serves 4

While pasta is never served hot on the Italian table, rice can be prepared hot or cold, as it retains its firm texture even when marinated in an acidic dressing. This is one of the rice salads I make in summer. Short-grain rice is starchy and heavy—not characteristics we want in a salad. If you toast the rice before cooking, the grains will remain separate and firm. In addition, rinsing it well under cold running water after cooking removes excess starch, giving the rice definition in combination with the other ingredients.

1 CUP MEDIUM-GRAIN RICE

KOSHER SALT

¼ CUP WHITE WINE VINEGAR

1 POUND RAW MEDIUM SHRIMP, IN THEIR SHELLS

1 WHOLE HOT RED PEPPER, SEEDED

⅓ CUP TOASTED PINE NUTS

6 TABLESPOONS MINCED FRESH FLAT-LEAF PARSLEY

2 TABLESPOONS FRESH BASIL, MINCED

FOR THE DRESSING

JUICE OF 1 LEMON, OR TO TASTE

1 SHALLOT, MINCED

SEA SALT

½ CUP EXTRA-VIRGIN OLIVE OIL, OR TO TASTE

1. Preheat an oven to 350°F. Spread the rice out on a sheet pan. Slide it on the middle rack of the oven to toast, 3 to 4 minutes. Allow to cool.

2. In the meantime, in a large pot, bring to a boil enough water to cover the shrimp. Add 3 teaspoons salt and the vinegar. Drop in the shrimp and the hot red pepper and cover. Bring to a boil over high heat, stirring occasionally, until the shrimp are just cooked through, about 3 minutes. They should be pink on the surface and opaque inside. Drain, reserving the cooking water but discard the pepper. Cool and then shell, removing the tails.

3. Strain the shrimp stock. Add enough water to make 4 quarts. Bring it to a boil and stir in the rice and 1 tablespoon salt. Boil until tender but firm to the bite, about 15 minutes, depending on the rice. Rinse immediately in cold running water until it runs clear. Drain well and spread out on a clean kitchen towel to dry.

4. In a salad bowl, make the dressing: Combine the lemon juice, shallot, and sea salt to taste. Whisk in the olive oil in a slow stream. Add the rice, shrimp, pine nuts, parsley, and basil. Check for seasoning and serve at once.

AHEAD-OF-TIME NOTE: The salad can be made 3 hours in advance. It is best if it is not refrigerated before serving. The lemon juice should be added just before serving.

PUGLIESE RICE SALAD
WITH MANY PICKLED VEGETABLES

Serves 8 to 10

My Roman-born friend Anna Maria Erenbourg Weld spends her summers in Puglia, where she learned how to make this exceptional, complex, and tangy rice salad filled with the region's celebrated pickled vegetables, *sott'aceti* in Italian. It is typically made in a large quantity for big family gatherings because the terrific variety of ingredients it contains makes it impractical for a small batch. Consider it for entertaining or special occasions when expecting a large gathering. Success will depend largely on the quality of the pickled vegetables and other ingredients you use. The best are genuine Italian mixed *sott'aceti* imported from Italy. See Rice and Shrimp Salad (page 48) for notes on selecting and cooking rice for salads.

1 POUND MEDIUM-GRAIN RICE

2 TABLESPOONS KOSHER SALT

1 LEMON, SLICED IN HALF

1 POUND CACIOCAVALLO, OR FRESH MOZZARELLA, DICED

½ CUP GAETA OLIVES, RINSED, PITTED, AND HALVED

½ CUP PICKLED EGGPLANT, DRAINED

½ CUP TINY PICKLED ONIONS, DRAINED

½ CUP MIXED ITALIAN PICKLED VEGETABLES, DRAINED

½ CUP PICKLED ROASTED ARTICHOKES

½ CUP PORCINI MUSHROOMS PRESERVED IN OLIVE OIL, DRAINED

½ CUP PICKLED ROASTED PEPPERS, DRAINED

½ CUP CAPERS, DRAINED

1 CUP SWEET, VINE-RIPENED CHERRY TOMATOES, HALVED

6 HARD-BOILED EGGS, SLICED

3 7-OUNCE CANS ITALIAN TUNA PRESERVED IN OLIVE OIL, DRAINED AND FLAKED

5 TABLESPOONS CHOPPED FRESH MINT

EXTRA-VIRGIN OLIVE OIL, TO TASTE

YELLOW MUSTARD, TO TASTE

SEA SALT AND FRESHLY GROUND BLACK PEPPER

1 CUP HOMEMADE MAYONNAISE (PAGE 218)

1. Preheat an oven to 350°F. Spread the rice out on a sheet pan. Slide it on the middle rack of the oven to toast, 3 to 4 minutes. Allow to cool.

2. In a kettle, bring 5 quarts water to a rapid boil. Add the salt and lemon halves. Boil until the rice is cooked but firm to the bite, about 15 minutes. Drain at once and rinse thoroughly in cold running water until it runs clear. Drain again. Spread the rice out on a clean kitchen towel to dry.

3. In an ample serving bowl, combine the cooked rice with all the other ingredients. Toss well and serve.

AHEAD-OF-TIME NOTE: You may prepare the rice salad several hours in advance.

WARM SALT COD AND POTATO SALAD

Serves 4 to 6

I love the un-fishy flavor and chewy texture of salt cod, *baccalà* in Italian. Like so many Italians, I grew up eating it. My mother often made it on Christian days of abstinence, but she always varied the recipe. It might have been a tomato stew specked with dry-cured black olives, a "white" version with potatoes and green olives, or, in summer, a room-temperature salad like this one. Select the skinless and boneless variety of *baccalà*, which eliminates tedious and unnecessary preparation. Look for meaty, creamy-colored fillets and avoid excessively thin, brown pieces. The dressing used here is also typically used for salads of freshly cooked fish fillets or boiled crabmeat. A richer alternative is Light Lemon Mayonnaise (page 218).

1½ POUNDS SKINLESS, BONELESS BACCALÀ

THICK APPLE SLICE OR ½ POTATO

½ POUND YUKON GOLD OR EASTERN BOILING POTATOES

5 TABLESPOONS EXTRA-VIRGIN OLIVE OIL, OR TO TASTE

3 TABLESPOONS FRESHLY SQUEEZED LEMON JUICE, OR TO TASTE

1 MEDIUM CLOVE GARLIC, FINELY CHOPPED

FRESHLY GROUND BLACK PEPPER

FINE SEA SALT

3 TABLESPOONS CHOPPED FRESH FLAT-LEAF PARSLEY

1. To prepare the salt cod, place it in a bowl and add cold water to cover and the apple or potato, which helps to draw out the salt. Refrigerate overnight, changing the water several times. Drain the salt cod and rinse in fresh cool water.

2. Place the cod in a pan with cold water to cover. Bring to a boil, then reduce the heat and cook gently until tender but not falling apart, 15 to 20 minutes. Taste before draining to make sure it is cooked. If it is still too hard, continue cooking it gently. If it is still too salty, cover with fresh cold water, bring to a boil again, and drain and rinse under cold water. Drain well and pat dry with a cotton kitchen towel. Check for any skin and bones that may have been missed. Break up the fish into large flakes and transfer to a serving plate.

3. In a separate pan, place the potatoes with cold water to cover by 2 inches. Bring to a boil, then reduce to medium-low and cook until tender, about 22 to 30 minutes, depending on the size of the potatoes. When cool enough to handle, peel them. Cut the potatoes in half and cut into ¼-inch slices.

4. In a small bowl stir together the oil, lemon juice, garlic, and pepper to taste. Drizzle over the fish and potatoes. Add salt to taste and sprinkle with the parsley. Serve at room temperature.

FAST-DAY SALAD WITH
TUNA, POTATOES, EGGS, AND ASPARAGUS

Serves 4

Canned Italian tuna fillets packed in olive oil are a marvelous product with a myriad of uses in the Italian kitchen. Called *ventresca*, it comes from the underside of the bonito tuna, which is light pink, moist, and delicate in comparison to the dry white-meat albacore variety that is packed for the American market. It is a delight in composed salads such as this one. There are many variations of *antipasto di magro,* so-called because there is no meat in it. *Magro* means "lean," a term often assigned to dishes served on Christian fast days. While the salad can be served with extra-virgin olive oil and good red wine vinegar, I find the dressing that most people like best is the Light Lemon Mayonnaise on page 218.

½ POUND (5 SMALL) FINGERLING, YUKON GOLD, OR OTHER BOILING POTATOES

3 EGGS

½ POUND TENDER ASPARAGUS IN SEASON

1 TEASPOON SEA SALT

1 CAN (6½ OUNCES) IMPORTED ITALIAN TUNA BELLY FILLETS IN OLIVE OIL, DRAINED AND ROUGHLY FLAKED

2 TABLESPOONS THINLY SLIVERED RED ONION, ABOUT 1 INCH LONG

HALF RECIPE LIGHT LEMON MAYONNAISE (PAGE 218)

1 TABLESPOON DRAINED SMALL CAPERS

1. Put the unpeeled potatoes in a pot with enough cold water to cover and bring to a boil over high heat. Immediately reduce the heat to medium and cook until tender when pierced with a sharp knife, about 20 minutes. Drain and when cool enough to handle, peel the potatoes and cut them crosswise into ¼-inch-thick slices.

2. In the meantime, place the eggs in a saucepan with cold water to cover and bring to a boil. Cook them for a total of 15 minutes from the time they are placed on the stove. Drain and peel while still warm so that they will slip out of their shells easily, then allow to cool before cutting crosswise into ¼-inch-thick slices.

3. Remove the tough lower stalk of the asparagus. Fill another saucepan with water and bring to a boil. Add the salt, then the asparagus. Boil, uncovered, until tender, about 7 minutes. Drain, refresh in cold water, and set aside. It is best if they are still warm when dressed.

4. In a salad bowl, preferably of clear glass, layer first the potatoes, then the tuna, onion, asparagus, and eggs, spooning a little mayonnaise on each layer before arranging the next one. Spoon more mayonnaise on top and scatter on the capers. Serve within 2 hours of preparing.

GREEN BEAN AND POTATO SALAD
WITH PARSLEY AND BASIL

Serves 4

My aunt Rita's simple and lovely classic Italian summer salad is especially good with garden-fresh green beans, which should be cooked until tender for maximum sweetness and flavor. An "al dente" texture should only be used for dried pasta cooking—not for most vegetables. For a creamy dressing, use Homemade Mayonnaise (page 218) thinned with a few tablespoons of white wine vinegar or lemon juice. Or make the vinaigrette dressing below.

1 POUND FINGERLING, YUKON GOLD, RED BLISS, OR OTHER BOILING POTATOES

1 POUND FRESH YOUNG GREEN BEANS

1 TEASPOON COARSE SALT

1 RED ONION, SLICED THIN AND CHOPPED

4 TABLESPOONS CHOPPED FRESH FLAT-LEAF PARSLEY

4 TABLESPOONS FRESH BASIL CUT INTO CHIFFONADE

VINAIGRETTE DRESSING

½ CUP EXTRA-VIRGIN OLIVE OIL

1 TEASPOON DIJON MUSTARD

¼ CUP WHITE WINE VINEGAR

1 TEASPOON SEA SALT

½ TEASPOON FRESHLY GROUND WHITE PEPPER

4 FRESHLY BOILED HARD-COOKED EGGS, CUT INTO QUARTERS

1. Place the potatoes in a pan with enough cold water to cover. Bring to a boil and cook over medium heat until tender. (Cooking time will vary based on the size of the potatoes, but count on at least 20 minutes.) Drain and refresh under cold water for several seconds. When cool enough to handle, peel if using the white variety. Fingerling or Red Bliss do not need to be peeled. Cut into slices ¼ inch thick.

2. Trim the stems off the beans but leave the tapered tip intact. Bring enough water to cover to a rapid boil. Add the beans and salt. Cook until tender but not too soft or crunchy, 6 to 9 minutes depending on their size and freshness. Drain and run under cold water to refresh. Drain again.

3. Combine the ingredients for the vinaigrette dressing and mix well. Taste for seasoning.

4. Select an ample bowl and add 2 tablespoons of the dressing. Lay the potato slices on top. Sprinkle with the onion. Arrange the green beans and the eggs over that. Pour additional dressing to taste over the top, then scatter with the parsley and basil. Serve warm or at room temperature.

VARIATION: Add 1 fennel bulb, stalks trimmed, halved, cored, and cut into 2-inch slices, to the cooking water with the green beans.

CAULIFLOWER SALAD
WITH CAPERS, SCALLIONS, AND LEMON

Serves 6

This classic vegetable salad, piquant from the generous dressing of capers, olives, and lemon, was a staple of my childhood. I have varied the way I make it over the years, sometimes adding cornichons and different herbs, but my friends and family seem always to love this version best.

1 LARGE HEAD CAULIFLOWER

1 TABLESPOON SALT

JUICE OF ½ LEMON

FOR THE DRESSING

3 TABLESPOONS DRAINED SMALL CAPERS
OR COARSELY CHOPPED LARGE CAPERS

¼ CUP PITTED GAETA OLIVES,
CUT INTO QUARTERS

1 BUNCH SCALLIONS, WHITE PART AND
1 INCH OF GREEN ONLY, THINLY SLICED

2 TABLESPOONS CHOPPED FRESH
FLAT-LEAF PARSLEY

¼ CUP EXTRA-VIRGIN OLIVE OIL,
OR TO TASTE

3 TABLESPOONS FRESHLY SQUEEZED
LEMON JUICE, OR MORE TO TASTE

SALT AND FRESHLY GROUND
BLACK PEPPER

1. Pour enough water into a saucepan to cover the cauliflower generously and bring it to a boil. Meanwhile, trim the stalks off the cauliflower and cut off the hard base and discard. Remove the core and separate the cauliflower into florets. Add the cauliflower to the boiling water along with the salt and lemon juice (the lemon juice will help the cauliflower to retain its color). Cover, return to a boil, and continue to cook until the cauliflower is tender but not mushy, 5 to 7 minutes. Take care, as cauliflower goes from undercooked to overcooked very quickly.

2. Meanwhile, in a small bowl combine all the dressing ingredients, including salt and pepper to taste. Whisk to blend.

3. When the cauliflower is cooked, drain it, immediately plunge it into cold water to stop further cooking, and drain again. While it is still warm, toss it with the dressing in a salad bowl. Adjust seasoning for taste and serve.

FARRO SALAD
WITH CHERRY TOMATOES, FRESH MOZZARELLA, AND HERBS

Serves 4

Farro, or emmer in English, has long been comfort food for the Italians and other people living near the Mediterranean. I like its chewy texture and nutty flavor best in salads such as this one.

1 CUP WHOLE FARRO

2 TABLESPOONS FRESHLY SQUEEZED LEMON JUICE

⅓ CUP EXTRA-VIRGIN OLIVE OIL

SEA SALT AND FRESHLY GROUND BLACK PEPPER

2 OUNCES FRESH MOZZARELLA CHEESE, DRAINED AND DICED

1 CUP SWEET VINE-RIPENED CHERRY TOMATOES, HALVED

¼ CUP COMBINED FINELY CHOPPED FRESH BASIL, FLAT-LEAF PARSLEY, MARJORAM, AND CHIVES

1. Rinse the farro in cold water and pick out any impurities. Cover with cold water and allow it to soak for 1 hour. Drain.

2. Bring 2 quarts of water to a boil in a medium saucepan. Add the farro. Reduce the heat, cover, and simmer, stirring from time to time, for 45 minutes or until the farro is tender. Remove from the heat and allow the grains to swell in the cooking water for 10 minutes, then drain.

3. While the farro is cooking, make the dressing. Whisk together the lemon juice, olive oil, and salt and pepper to taste.

4. In a serving dish, combine the farro, cheese, tomatoes, herbs, and dressing. Toss together, and serve warm or at room temperature.

SWEET AND SOUR ROASTED BEET SALAD
WITH ORANGE AND MINT

Serves 4

Everyone who likes beets loves this dish. Its origins are in my family, but it has evolved in my own kitchen over the years. Red wine vinegar and good olive oil is a classic dressing, but I find that beets, with their natural sweetness, cry out for a sweet-and-sour treatment. I boil industrial-variety balsamic vinegar to a fruity, tart syrup and temper it with olive oil. The addition of oranges provides a burst of sweetness and a pleasant acidity.

10 SMALL TO MEDIUM BEETS

3 NAVEL ORANGES

FOR THE DRESSING

½ CUP BALSAMIC VINEGAR

4 TABLESPOONS EXTRA-VIRGIN OLIVE OIL

1 TABLESPOON CHOPPED FRESH MINT LEAVES

1. Preheat an oven to 400°F.

2. Trim the leaves off the beets, but do not cut into the root. Transfer to a sheet pan and slide them onto the middle rack of the oven. Roast until tender, 30 to 45 minutes, depending on the freshness of the beets. When you can pierce them easily with a sharp knife, they are done. When they are cool enough to handle, slice off the stem stub and slip off their skins. Slice and set aside.

3. Grate the zest from one of the oranges. Using a small sharp knife, cut off the peel and white pith from all the oranges. Working over a large bowl, cut between the membranes to release the orange segments. Set aside.

4. Meanwhile, simmer the balsamic vinegar in a small pot until it is reduced to ¼ cup, then pass it through a small sieve to remove any sediment. Mix the olive oil and orange zest in a small bowl and stir in the reduced balsamic vinegar . In a serving bowl, arrange the beets and orange sections. Spoon the dressing over the salad and scatter the mint leaves on top. Serve.

AHEAD-OF-TIME NOTE: This entire dish can be prepared a day in advance with the exception of adding the mint. Cover and refrigerate. Bring to room temperature and scatter the mint on top before serving.

MY GRANDMOTHER'S
WHOLE-WHEAT BREAD SALAD

Serves 4

This heirloom recipe was passed down from my paternal grandmother, who learned it when her life as an immigrant was so hard and there was little else to eat besides stale bread. Despite its most humble origins, this salad is delicious. The bread must be coarse artisan bread. Other breads will not hold up to being dressed with oil and vinegar, or combined with watery tomatoes. High-quality extra-virgin olive oil is indispensable.

½ LOAF (ABOUT 1 POUND) 2- TO 3-DAY-OLD COARSE PEASANT BREAD OR STURDY ITALIAN-STYLE BREAD, CRUSTS REMOVED

1 LARGE CLOVE GARLIC, CUT IN HALF

6 TABLESPOONS WATER, OR MORE, DEPENDING UPON THE DRYNESS OF THE BREAD

½ CUP EXTRA-VIRGIN OLIVE OIL

3 TABLESPOONS RED WINE VINEGAR

2 LARGE, VINE-RIPENED TOMATOES OR 4 PLUM TOMATOES, SEEDED AND DICED, OR 1 PINT SWEET CHERRY TOMATOES, CUT IN HALF

HALF A VIDALIA ONION, OR RED ONION, QUARTERED AND SLICED PAPER-THIN

2 TABLESPOONS TORN FRESH BASIL

2 TEASPOONS CHOPPED FRESH OREGANO LEAVES, OR 1 TEASPOON DRIED OREGANO

4 TABLESPOONS CHOPPED FRESH FLAT-LEAF PARSLEY

½ TEASPOON SALT, OR TO TASTE

¼ TEASPOON FRESHLY GROUND BLACK PEPPER, OR TO TASTE

1. Slice the bread and rub the slices with garlic on both sides; discard the garlic. Tear or cut the bread into 1-inch pieces. You should have approximately 6 cups. Place in a shallow bowl and sprinkle evenly with the 6 tablespoons of water. If the bread is very dry, you may need to add another 1 or 2 tablespoons of water.

2. In a separate bowl, stir together the olive oil, vinegar, tomatoes, onion, and half of the herbs. Let marinate for 10 minutes. Pour over the bread, add the remaining herbs, and toss well. Season with the salt and pepper and serve.

AHEAD-OF-TIME NOTE: This salad can be made 1 or 2 hours in advance as long as a sturdy bread is used.

BREAD SALAD WITH ROASTED PEPPERS

Serves 4 to 6

The success of this salad depends on the quality of bread. It should contain no sugar, eggs, or seeds, and it must be chewy and substantial in order to stand up to the dressing. Three- or four-day-old sourdough or sturdy peasant bread will do nicely. Very airy, unsubstantial bread will become soggy very quickly upon contact with the dressing. Season with plenty of black pepper, a nice contrast to the sweetness of the roasted bell peppers.

2 LARGE RED BELL PEPPERS, OR A COMBINATION OF RED AND YELLOW PEPPERS

1-POUND LOAF STURDY ITALIAN BREAD OR PEASANT BREAD

½ CUP EXTRA-VIRGIN OLIVE OIL

¼ CUP WHITE WINE VINEGAR

½ CUP WATER

1 SMALL RED OR WHITE ONION, QUARTERED AND VERY FINELY SLICED, OR ½ CUP VERY FINELY SLICED VIDALIA ONION

1 GREEN ONION, INCLUDING 4 INCHES OF GREEN, FINELY SLICED

2 TABLESPOONS BRINE-CURED, PITTED, AND SLICED SHARPLY FLAVORED IMPORTED GREEN OLIVES SUCH AS PICHOLINE OR SICILIAN OLIVES

1 TABLESPOON CHOPPED FRESH OREGANO OR 1 TEASPOON DRIED OREGANO

½ TEASPOON SALT

¼ TEASPOON FRESHLY GROUND BLACK PEPPER, OR MORE TO TASTE

1. First roast the peppers: Arrange the peppers on a grill rack above a charcoal fire, or on wire racks positioned over the burners of a gas or electric stove, or 2 to 3 inches under a preheated broiler, or in an oven preheated to 450°F. Roast them until they are charred all over and tender inside, turning them frequently to ensure they cook evenly, about 25 minutes in the oven but less time by the other methods. Remove them from the heat. When the peppers are cool enough to handle, using a sharp knife, cut them in half vertically. Remove the stem and lift off the skin, then remove all of the seeds. Cut the peppers into 2-inch strips.

2. While the peppers are roasting, prepare the bread and the dressing. Remove all the crust from the bread and cut it into bite-size cubes. Measure out 5 cups; set any excess aside for some other purpose. In a bowl, combine the oil, vinegar, water, onions, olives, herbs, salt, and pepper. Allow the mixture to marinate for 10 minutes. Transfer the bread cubes and pepper strips to a salad bowl. Add the dressing and toss to unify the ingredients. Serve.

AHEAD-OF-TIME NOTE: Because the bread increasingly absorbs the dressing after the salad is made, it is best served within several hours.

WARM WINTER GREENS SALAD
WITH BACON VINAIGRETTE

Serves 4

Like most vegetables, salad greens are seasonal in the Italian kitchen. While summer brings soft lettuces and sun-drenched tomatoes, the cool weather brings radicchio and spinach. And what better dressing for these more assertive greens than the smoky bacon, olive oil, and vinegar treatment of the Italians?

2 TABLESPOONS OLIVE OR GRAPE SEED OIL

4 THICK SLICES BACON, CUT INTO ¼-INCH STRIPS

1 MEDIUM SHALLOT, MINCED

2 TABLESPOONS RED WINE VINEGAR

PINCH OF SUGAR

1 TABLESPOON DIJON MUSTARD

¼ CUP EXTRA-VIRGIN OLIVE OIL

5 OUNCES WINTER LETTUCE, SUCH AS MÂCHE, GEM, SPINACH, OR RADICCHIO, OR A COMBINATION

SALT AND FRESHLY GROUND BLACK PEPPER

1. In an ample skillet, warm the 2 tablespoons oil. Add the bacon strips and cook over medium heat until browned and crisp, about 5 minutes. Take the skillet off the heat and transfer the bacon to a dish and set aside. Stir in the shallot, vinegar, sugar, mustard, and extra-virgin olive oil. Using a rubber spatula to scrape it out, transfer the dressing to a large salad bowl.

2. Add the greens to the bowl and toss with the dressing. Transfer to individual serving dishes, season with salt and pepper, and top with the reserved bacon strips. Serve at once.

COLD SEARED BEEF SALAD
WITH HERBS, CAPERS, AND LEMON DRESSING
Serves 4

Leftover meat never goes to waste in my kitchen. The Italians have many inventive uses for it, exemplified in this superb family recipe for beef salad. It is so good, you need not wait for the opportunity of leftover beef to make it. I use charcoal-broiled flank, skirt, or sirloin steak for this salad, although care should be taken to cut the meat into very thin slices.

1 POUND GRILLED, ROASTED, OR BOILED BEEF, TRIMMED OF FAT

FOR THE DRESSING

4 CORNICHONS, MINCED

1 TABLESPOON CHOPPED FRESH FLAT-LEAF PARSLEY

4 BASIL LEAVES, MINCED

3 TABLESPOONS DRAINED CAPERS, MINCED

½ TEASPOON FRESHLY GRATED LEMON ZEST

3 TABLESPOONS FRESHLY SQUEEZED LEMON JUICE

1 TEASPOON RED WINE VINEGAR

¼ CUP EXTRA-VIRGIN OLIVE OIL

1 GENEROUS TEASPOON DIJON MUSTARD

SALT AND FRESHLY GROUND BLACK PEPPER

1. Cut the meat into thin, finger-size pieces.

2. In a small bowl combine all the dressing ingredients, including salt and pepper to taste, and, using a fork, stir to mix. Pour the dressing over the beef and toss well. Taste for seasoning. Serve at room temperature.

AHEAD-OF-TIME NOTE: The dressing can be made 4 to 5 days in advance, covered, and refrigerated, then brought back to room temperature before using. Once the meat and dressing are combined, the salad can be refrigerated for several hours, or left at room temperature, covered, for 1 hour.

A BOWLFUL OF COMFORT:
SOUPS

One reason Italian food is so comforting is the custom of the long, slow meal with family and friends. Kinship and conviviality take time and besides, the most important discussions, whether about family, politics, or philosophy, take place at the table. And so Italians prefer a measured procession of many plates or courses instead of the too-efficient combining of vegetable, starch, and meat on a single plate. *Chi va piano va sano e lontano* ("If you go slow you get far and you get there in one piece") would be their mantra. Soup fits handily into this approach as an alternative to a pasta or risotto first course. Variety rules. A *zuppa* is weighty and chowder-like while a *minestra* is delicate, light, refined—a bit more substantial than a *brodo,* which may contain rice, tiny pasta grains, or meat dumplings, or nothing at all. Then there's *minestrone*—the suffix *-one* means "big"—thick with pasta, beans, and chunked vegetables. I've tried to include at least one of each in this chapter. Soup is soothing, or should be, and so in Italy it is served warm, not hot.

RICHLY FLAVORED CHICKEN SOUP
WITH "PEPPERCORN" PASTINA

Serves 6

Italians believe that chicken broth "opens the stomach" for the courses that follow during the meal. A proper chicken soup in my grandmother's kitchen consisted of clear broth made from free-range fowl from the family flock. The broth cooked for a long, slow simmer before it was strained; the idea was not to distract from its rich, clear flavor with too many vegetables or other ingredients. A handful of tiny soup pasta, a scattering of Pecorino cheese, and a sprinkling of chopped parsley was the finishing touch. This recipe differs from the basic Chicken Broth on page 214 in that a whole chicken is cooked and the meat is served as a second course accompanied by a dressing, my favorite being homemade mayonnaise mixed with capers and chopped fresh herbs, or mayonnaise blended with horseradish (see page 218).

1 4-POUND FREE-RANGE CHICKEN

1 YELLOW ONION, UNPEELED, HALVED

1 CARROT, SCRAPED AND CUT IN HALF

1 LARGE CELERY STALK, INCLUDING LEAVES

1 LARGE FENNEL STALK, INCLUDING LEAVES (OPTIONAL)

¼-POUND PIECE CELERY ROOT (CELERIAC), SLICED

1 BAY LEAF

HANDFUL OF FRESH FLAT-LEAF PARSLEY

1 TOMATO, FRESH OR CANNED

1 TABLESPOON WHOLE BLACK OR WHITE PEPPERCORNS

SEA SALT

⅓ CUP ACINI DI PEPPE ("PEPPERCORN") PASTINA, OTHER SOUP PASTINA SUCH AS SEMI DI MELLONE ("MELON SEEDS"), OR ORZO ("BARLEY"), OR 4 OUNCES FINE ANGEL'S HAIR PASTA

FRESHLY GRATED AGED PARMIGIANO-REGGIANO OR GRANA PADANO CHEESE, FOR SERVING

1. Wash the chicken. Put all the ingredients up to but not including the salt in an 8-quart stockpot and cover with no more than 1½ inches water. Cover the pot and bring to a boil. Immediately lower to a gentle simmer and cook, partially covered, until the meat is cooked through, about 1½ hours. Skim the foam whenever it forms on the top. The broth should cook gently for the entire cooking time, never returning to a boil.

2. When the chicken is cooked, transfer to a side bowl with some of the broth to keep it moist and cover. When ready to serve, remove the skin, cut the breast meat into thin slices, and pass a dressing as suggested above.

3. To make the soup, skim off as much fat from the broth as you can. Strain through a fine sieve. When ready to serve, return the broth to a clean pot, bring to a boil, and add the salt and the pasta. Simmer over medium heat until al dente. Taste for seasoning. Ladle into soup bowls, sprinkle with grated cheese, and serve hot.

WEDDING SOUP

Serves 10

There is much confusion about the authentic way of making Italian wedding soup because there are as many versions as there are brides. Once transported to America, home cooks put a new spin on what they cooked, making any culinary pedigree that much more removed. This is a recipe with origins in Sardinia. The little meat dumplings in the soup are called *bombetti,* "little bombs," for their shape, but the comparison ends there. They are, in fact, very light and delicate. This is a luxurious soup, rich with tender meats and meatballs, pasta, and greens.

FOR THE BROTH

1 RECIPE TASTY MEAT BROTH (PAGE 213), STRAINED

3½ POUNDS BEEF FLANKEN (OR SHORT RIBS)

FOR THE BOMBETTE

1 TABLESPOON EXTRA-VIRGIN OLIVE OIL

1 ONION, MINCED

1¼ POUNDS GROUND VEAL

¼ POUND BOILED HAM, MINCED

½ POUND EASTERN OR YUKON GOLD POTATOES, BOILED, PEELED, AND MASHED

1 EXTRA-LARGE EGG, BEATEN

GRATED ZEST OF 1 LEMON

2 TEASPOONS FRESH MINCED THYME OR 1 TEASPOON DRIED THYME

2 TABLESPOONS MINCED FRESH FLAT-LEAF PARSLEY

¼ CUP FRESHLY GRATED PECORINO ROMANO OR PARMIGIANO-REGGIANO CHEESE

GENEROUS TWIST OF FRESHLY GROUND BLACK PEPPER

1½ TEASPOONS SEA SALT

1 CUP FREGULA (SEE PAGE 88) OR OTHER SOUP PASTINA SUCH AS *SEMI DI MELLONE* "MELON SEEDS"

2 CUPS SWISS CHARD, RIBS REMOVED AND CHOPPED

1. In an ample soup kettle, combine the broth with the beef flanken. Bring to a boil, then reduce to a simmer. Cook until the beef is tender and falling off the bone, about 2½ hours, skimming frequently. Cool the broth and skim off the fat.

2. Meanwhile, warm the olive oil in a medium skillet over medium heat and sauté the onion until wilted, about 6 minutes.

3. In a bowl, combine the sautéed onion, veal, ham, mashed potatoes, egg, lemon zest, thyme, parsley, grated cheese, pepper, and salt. Use your hands to mix well. Form the mixture into little oval-shaped balls about the size of pecans.

4. Bring the broth to a boil again. Add the meatballs and the fregula, if using, and simmer over medium heat, partially covered, until the pasta is 2 minutes short of cooking. If using pastina, check the package instructions for cooking time. Add the Swiss chard and cook for 2 minutes more. Taste for seasoning and serve at once.

CLASSIC MINESTRONE

Serves 8 to 10

The secret to the success of this colorful, meatless vegetable soup is the use of fresh vegetables, high quality extra-virgin olive oil, and authentic Parmigiano-Reggiano cheese. A *battuto* (chopped mixture) of garlic, rosemary, and parsley at the last minute lends extra flavor. Or stir a few tablespoons of Basil Pesto (page 44) into the soup just before serving.

3 TABLESPOONS EXTRA-VIRGIN OLIVE OIL, PLUS ADDITIONAL FOR SERVING

3 CANNED PLUM TOMATOES, SEEDED AND MINCED, PLUS ¼ CUP OF THEIR JUICES

1 LARGE ONION, COARSELY CHOPPED

1 POTATO, PEELED AND DICED

1 LARGE CELERY STALK, WITH THE LEAVES, CHOPPED

¾ POUND BUTTERNUT SQUASH, DICED

2 TEASPOONS FRESH ROSEMARY, OR 1 TEASPOON DRIED ROSEMARY, PLUS 3 TABLESPOONS CHOPPED FRESH ROSEMARY OR 2 TABLESPOONS DRIED ROSEMARY

3 TABLESPOONS MINCED FRESH FLAT-LEAF PARSLEY LEAVES AND STEMS, PLUS ANOTHER 3 TABLESPOONS

1 LARGE CARROT, SCRAPED AND DICED

½ POUND GREEN CABBAGE, FINELY SHREDDED (ABOUT 1½ CUPS)

1 POUND FRESH CRANBERRY BEANS, SHELLED (1 TO 1½ CUPS), OR 2 CUPS CANNED PINTO, PINK, OR SMALL WHITE BEANS, RINSED AND DRAINED

3 QUARTS WATER

2 TABLESPOONS SALT, OR TO TASTE

FRESHLY GROUND BLACK PEPPER

¼ POUND GREEN BEANS, CUT INTO 1-INCH LENGTHS

2 SMALL ZUCCHINI, DICED

1½ CUPS CAULIFLOWER FLORETS

1 CUP CONCHIGLIETTE ("LITTLE SHELLS") OR DITALINI ("LITTLE THIMBLES") PASTA

4 LARGE CLOVES GARLIC, FINELY CHOPPED

FRESHLY GRATED PARMIGIANO-REGGIANO CHEESE, FOR SERVING

1. In a large pot, combine the olive oil, tomatoes and juice, onion, potato, celery, squash, the 2 teaspoons rosemary, the 3 tablespoons parsley, the carrot, cabbage, cranberry beans (reserve canned beans, if using), water, salt, and pepper. Cover and bring to a boil over high heat. Immediately reduce the heat to medium-low, partially cover, and simmer for about 40 minutes, or until the beans are cooked.

2. Add the green beans, zucchini, cauliflower, and pasta and cook for 8 minutes. Stir in the garlic, the 3 tablespoons rosemary, and the 3 tablespoons parsley; if using canned beans, add them at this point. Continue cooking the soup, uncovered, over medium heat, until the pasta is not quite al dente, about 8 minutes.

3. Serve the soup with abundant freshly grated cheese, a dribble of olive oil, and a generous twist of pepper to taste.

CARROT AND FENNEL SOUP

Serves 4 to 6

Making vegetable soup without added stocks of any kind delivers the true essence of natural flavors. This is how you can do it without insipid results. If you like the flavors of carrot and fennel, that's what you'll get here, unadulterated. If you have a food processor with a slicing attachment, you can slice the vegetables in no time at all rather than cutting them by hand. The last step—passing the pureed soup through a food mill or sieve—produces a smooth, silky texture.

1 HEAD FRESH FENNEL

4 TABLESPOONS UNSALTED BUTTER OR
EXTRA-VIRGIN OLIVE OIL, OR A
COMBINATION

1 ONION, SLICED

1½ POUNDS CARROTS, SCRAPED AND
SLICED INTO THIN ROUNDS

8 CUPS WATER

2 TEASPOONS SEA SALT

FRESHLY GROUND WHITE PEPPER

1. Trim the tough, dark stalks off the fennel and split the bulb in half lengthwise. Cut out the tough inner core and cut the white stalks into thin slices. Chop and reserve the tender lighter green fronds.

2. In a soup kettle, warm the butter or olive oil, or a mixture of both, if using. Stir in the sliced fennel, onion, and carrots and sauté over medium heat until the vegetables are softened and aromatic, about 15 minutes, stirring occasionally to prevent browning or sticking. Add the water and salt and simmer until the vegetables are completely soft, about 40 minutes. Use an immersion blender to thoroughly puree the mixture. Alternatively, allow it to cool somewhat and puree it in a jar blender two cups at a time.

3. For a silky texture, pass the soup through a food mill fitted with an attachment with the smallest holes. Alternatively, press the soup through a fine sieve. If you prefer a chunkier soup, serve it as is. Check for salt and add pepper to taste. Sprinkle with the chopped fennel fronds and serve.

CAULIFLOWER SOUP
WITH TINY PASTA SHELLS

Serves 6

Cauliflower, with its earthy flavor and exceptional nutritional benefits, is excellent in soups. The Italian way is to combine it with other vegetables in a nourishing, chunky potage (cream is not typically used in Italian soups). This is one of the soups I grew up on that remains a standard in my kitchen.

1 HEAD CAULIFLOWER

2 TABLESPOONS EXTRA-VIRGIN OLIVE OIL

2 OUNCES LEAN PANCETTA OR SALT PORK, CUT INTO SMALL DICE

1 ONION, MINCED

3 CLOVES GARLIC, BRUISED

1 TEASPOON MINCED FRESH ROSEMARY OR ½ TEASPOON CRUSHED DRIED ROSEMARY

1 CUP CHOPPED FRESH OR CANNED TOMATOES

1 TEASPOON SEA SALT

6 CUPS CHICKEN BROTH (PAGE 214), VEGETABLE BROTH (PAGE 215), OR WATER

1 MEDIUM POTATO, PEELED AND CUT INTO SMALL DICE

½ CUP CONCHIGLIETTE (TINY PASTA SHELLS)

FRESHLY GROUND BLACK PEPPER

FRESHLY GRATED PARMIGIANO-REGGIANO, GRANA PADANO, OR PECORINO *CHEESE*

1. Trim the cauliflower and remove the tough core. Separate the head into small florets.

2. In a large saucepan, warm the olive oil over medium heat and add the pancetta or salt pork. Sauté until colored, 4 minutes. Lower the heat to medium-low and add the onion and garlic; continue to sauté until softened, 4 minutes. Add the cauliflower and rosemary; sauté an additional 5 minutes. Add the tomatoes, sea salt, and 6 cups broth or water. Bring to a boil. Simmer, partially covered, for 15 minutes. Add the potato and simmer for 10 minutes. Add the pasta and simmer for an additional 6 minutes. Check for salt and add pepper. Serve with grated cheese to pass at the table.

SPICY TOMATO SOUP
WITH PANCETTA, SAFFRON, AND PARMESAN CRUSTS

Serves 4

A hint I picked up from the home cooks of Parma, where Parmigiano-Reggiano cheese is made, is that the rinds of Parmigiano-Reggiano or Grana Padano cheeses have many uses, particularly in soups where they can soak and soften, resulting in scrumptious little explosions of flavor. Once you taste this soup, you will never throw out another of these cheese rinds.

1 APPROXIMATE 2 X 3-INCH PIECE OF RIND FROM AUTHENTIC PARMIGIANO-REGGIANO OR GRANA PADANO CHEESE

3 TABLESPOONS EXTRA-VIRGIN OLIVE OIL

3 OUNCES PANCETTA, CHOPPED

1 ONION, MINCED

2 LARGE GARLIC CLOVES, CHOPPED

1 4-INCH STRIP LEMON ZEST, ABOUT ¾ INCH WIDE

SCANT ¼ TEASPOON DRIED RED PEPPER FLAKES

1 28-OUNCE CAN CRUSHED PLUM TOMATOES

1½ CUPS CHICKEN BROTH (PAGE 214)

1 TABLESPOON MINCED FRESH FLAT-LEAF PARSLEY

1 TEASPOON SEA SALT

2 ENVELOPES PURE SAFFRON POWDER, OR ¼ TEASPOON CRUMBLED SAFFRON THREADS

1. Preheat a toaster oven to 400°F or the "High" setting. Place the cheese rinds on a small sheet pan and warm them in the oven until they are easy to cut, about 5 minutes. Alternatively, zap them in a microwave oven for 20 seconds. Cut into very small dice and set aside.

2. In a soup kettle, warm the olive oil. Add the pancetta and sauté over medium heat until it is nicely browned and crisp, about 2 minutes. Use a slotted spoon to remove the pancetta from the pan and set aside. Add the onion, garlic, lemon zest, and red pepper flakes to the pan and sauté over medium-low heat until softened, about 6 minutes. Stir in the crushed tomatoes, chicken broth, and parsley. Simmer over medium-low heat until the mixture becomes condensed and aromatic, about 15 minutes.

3. Fish out the lemon zest and discard. Use an immersion blender to roughly puree the soup. Alternatively, allow the liquid to cool somewhat and transfer it to a a blender to puree. Return to the kettle and stir in the salt and saffron. Taste for seasoning. Bring the soup to the simmering point and drop in the diced cheese rinds. Turn off the heat to allow the rinds to soften. Ladle into individual soup bowls, scatter the surface with the reserved pancetta, and serve.

LENTIL SOUP
WITH CRUMBLED SAUSAGE AND DITALINI PASTA

Serves 4 to 6

I have never eaten a lentil soup better than this one I grew up on. It was one of my mother's winter supper inventions, which she alternated with versions substituting smoked sausage (like *luganega,* or if she couldn't get it, Polish- or Ukrainian-style kielbasa) for fresh, sweet pork and fennel sausage.

½ POUND (1½ CUPS) BROWN LENTILS

10 CUPS CHICKEN BROTH (PAGE 214) OR WATER

1 BAY LEAF

5 LINKS LEAN, SWEET FENNEL-FLAVORED ITALIAN PORK SAUSAGES

2 TABLESPOONS EXTRA-VIRGIN OLIVE OIL

6 LARGE CLOVES GARLIC, SMASHED

1 ONION, CHOPPED

1 LARGE CELERY STALK, INCLUDING LEAVES, CHOPPED

2 TEASPOONS FRESH THYME, MINCED, OR 1 TEASPOON DRIED THYME

3 TABLESPOONS TOMATO PASTE

1 16-OUNCE CAN PLUM TOMATOES, PEELED, SEEDED, AND CHOPPED, LIQUID RESERVED

½ CUP DITALINI ("LITTLE THIMBLE") PASTA

SEA SALT AND FRESHLY GROUND BLACK PEPPER

3 TABLESPOONS CHOPPED FRESH FLAT-LEAF PARSLEY

1. Pick over and wash the lentils in cold water. Transfer them to an ample pot, cover with the broth or water, and add the bay leaf. Bring to a boil, then immediately reduce to a simmer. Cook over medium-low heat until half-cooked, 10 minutes.

2. Meanwhile, slip the casings off the sausages. In an ample skillet, warm the olive oil. Brown the sausage meat over medium heat until lightly colored all over, about 7 minutes. Transfer to a side dish and drain any excess fat from the pan, leaving 3 tablespoons. Add the garlic, onion, celery, and thyme to the pan and sauté until the garlic is golden and the vegetables are softened and aromatic, about 5 minutes. Return the sausage to the pan. Dissolve the tomato paste in a little of the lentil broth and add it to the pan. Follow with the chopped tomatoes and their liquid. Simmer all together for 5 minutes.

3. Bring the lentils to a boil once again if they have cooled down. Transfer the skillet contents and the pasta to the pot with the boiling lentils. Simmer to marry the flavors, about 5 minutes. Add salt and pepper to taste. Turn off the heat, cover the pot, and allow the soup to rest until the pasta is fully cooked, about 4 more minutes. Discard the bay leaf, sprinkle with parsley, and serve.

MEATLESS PASTA and BEAN SOUP

Serves 4 to 6

Called *pasta e fagioli* in Italian, pasta and beans are a happy union. Each is a near-perfect food in itself, composed of energizing complex carbohydrates, proteins, vitamins, and minerals. There are endless types of pasta and bean soups in Italy. This is one of my favorite meatless versions that I learned from my Tuscan-bred friend, Flavia Destefanis. The key to making this meatless soup flavorful is using fruity olive oil, an intensely flavored *battuto,* or sautéed vegetable base, and fresh herbs.

4 OUNCES (⅔ CUP) DRIED CANNELLINI OR GREAT NORTHERN WHITE BEANS, RINSED AND PICKED OVER

6 TABLESPOONS EXTRA-VIRGIN OLIVE OIL

4 LARGE CLOVES GARLIC, CRUSHED

1 ONION, CHOPPED

1 CELERY STALK, WITH LEAVES, CHOPPED

1 CARROT, CHOPPED

4 TABLESPOONS MINCED FLAT-LEAF PARSLEY STEMS, PLUS 3 TABLESPOONS MINCED LEAVES

1 POUND VERY RIPE PLUM TOMATOES, PEELED, SEEDED, AND COARSELY CHOPPED, OR 1 16-OUNCE CAN PLUM TOMATOES, DRAINED, SEEDED, AND COARSELY CHOPPED

1½ TEASPOONS MINCED FRESH ROSEMARY

2 BAY LEAVES

4 OUNCES (1 CUP) DITALINI ("LITTLE THIMBLE") PASTA

SEA SALT AND FRESHLY GROUND BLACK PEPPER

1. To rehydrate the beans, put them in an ample bowl with cold water to cover by 3 inches. Let stand for 4 hours (or set aside at room temperature overnight). Alternatively, put the beans in a large saucepan with water to cover by 3 inches. Bring to a boil, cover, and remove from the heat. Let stand for 1 hour. Set aside.

2. To cook the beans, transfer them and their soaking water to an ample pot. Bring to a boil over high heat, then reduce the heat to medium. Cook halfway, about 30 minutes.

3. In the meantime, in a skillet, warm the olive oil over medium heat. Stir in the garlic, onion, celery, carrot, and parsley stems and sauté until the vegetables are soft and the onion transparent, about 15 minutes. Stir in the tomatoes, rosemary, and bay leaves. Simmer until the tomatoes release their juices, about 10 minutes.

4. Add the skillet contents to the pot with the beans and 1 quart of water. Partially cover the pot and simmer until the beans are cooked, about 30 minutes. If the soup looks like it is drying out as it cooks, add more water. (This is a thick, hearty soup, but it should still have some broth to it.)

5. Add the pasta and 2 teaspoons salt. Simmer until the pasta is just tender, about 8 minutes. Adjust for salt and add pepper and the chopped parsley. Discard the bay leaves and serve at once.

AHEAD OF TIME NOTE: To make in advance, prepare as directed but leave out the pasta. Once made, the soup can be cooled, covered, and refrigerated for up to 2 days. Cook the pasta separately in plenty of boiling salted water to cover. Drain and stir into the soup. Reheat gently and serve.

SAUSAGE AND GREENS SOUP

Serves 4

This homey soup can be made with various fresh greens, including kale, escarole, curly chicory, Swiss chard, or spinach. Chicken or turkey sausage can replace pork sausage, if preferred. If the broth is prepared in advance or stocked in the freezer, the soup is quick to make.

2 TABLESPOONS EXTRA-VIRGIN OLIVE OIL

1 ONION, MINCED

4 SWEET ITALIAN PORK SAUSAGE LINKS (ABOUT ¾ POUND), CASINGS REMOVED

¼ TEASPOON FRESHLY GROUND FENNEL SEEDS

2 CUPS WELL-WASHED CHOPPED FRESH KALE, RIBS REMOVED, OR OTHER GREENS, STEMMED

1 QUART CHICKEN BROTH (PAGE 214)

¾ CUP FARFALLETTE ("TINY BUTTERFLIES") OR OTHER SMALL SOUP PASTA

SEA SALT AND FRESHLY GROUND BLACK PEPPER

FRESHLY GRATED PARMIGIANO-REGGIANO OR GRANA PADANO CHEESE

In a soup kettle, warm the olive oil over medium heat. Add the onion, sausage meat, and fennel seeds and sauté until the meat is lightly colored and the onion is soft, about 7 minutes, stirring occasionally to break up the meat. Drain off any excess fat and add the greens to the pan; sauté until wilted, 1 minute. Add the broth, bring to a boil, and add the pasta. Reduce to a simmer and cook an additional 5 minutes. Taste and add salt and pepper. Serve with a generous sprinkling of grated cheese.

TUSCAN BREAD AND BEAN SOUP

Serves 4

This humble, homey soup is known as *zuppa lombarda* ("Lombard's Soup") in Tuscany, even though it has nothing to do with the northern Italian region of Lombardy. A Tuscan friend gave me the recipe years ago and it has become a standby in my family ever since. It must be made using dried, not canned, beans because the flavorful bean-cooking liquid becomes the broth for the soup.

1 CUPS DRIED CANNELLINI OR GREAT NORTHERN BEANS

6 LARGE CLOVES GARLIC, CRUSHED

1 SPRIG FRESH SAGE WITH 8 LEAVES

3 TABLESPOONS EXTRA-VIRGIN OLIVE OIL, PLUS MORE FOR DRIZZLING OVER SOUP

2 TEASPOONS SEA SALT

8 SLICES STALE CIABATTA BREAD, OR OTHER STURDY ARTISAN COUNTRY BREAD

FRESHLY GROUND BLACK PEPPER

1. Wash and pick over the dried beans. Put them in a pot with 5 cups cold water. Let stand overnight at room temperature, or up to 3 days, chilled. Alternatively, quick-soak the dried beans by putting them in a saucepan with 5 cups water. Bring to a boil, cover, remove from heat, and let stand for 1 hour.

2. Transfer the rehydrated beans with their soaking water to an ample pot. Add 5 of the garlic cloves, the sage sprig, and the 3 tablespoons olive oil. Bring to a boil and immediately reduce to a steady simmer. Cook gently over medium-low heat until the beans are tender, about 1 hour. There should be a ratio of about 1 part cooked beans to 2 parts bean stock. Add 2 teaspoons salt, cover, and set aside until the salt is absorbed, about 15 minutes. Taste and adjust salt to taste; fish out and discard the sage.

3. Toast the bread lightly; rub on both sides with the remaining garlic clove. Place two of the bread slices on the bottom of four individual soup bowls; drizzle with olive oil. Pour a ladleful of the hot beans and some of their liquid over each piece of bread. Sprinkle generously with freshly ground black pepper and drizzle with additional olive oil to taste. Serve at once.

5

PASTA BY HEART—
PLUS GRAIN, POLENTA, RICE, AND BEAN DISHES

Pasta, polenta, and beans are the comfort zone and foundation stone of Italian home cooking. Pasta is a national food, but its great importance is as a symbol of triumph over hunger in the poor south. The anthropologist Professor Folco Portinari says Italians rank it "somewhere between a sacrament and a psychotropic drug." Polenta and beans are regional. Before pasta, cheap, plentiful, and nutritious beans fed the common people. Pellegrino Artusi, author of the first national Italian cookbook, called them "the meat of the poor." Northern Italy's coarse-ground cornmeal, polenta, has similar stature: folklore tells of peasants who, given a rare ration of meat, stunned their benefactor by selling it to buy polenta. Of course: Meat would make a meal; polenta would feed a family. Here I include my favorite pasta, grain, polenta, and beans recipes, all of which have been passed down from generation to generation through grandmothers, aunts, or the ladies next door.

ZIETTA MARIEDDA'S
SAFFRON FREGULA

Makes 2 cups

My great aunt Maria ("Mariedda" in dialect) lived in Iglesias, an ancient mining city on the south coast of Sardinia that was founded by the Phoenicians. She made pasta at home every day until she was 102 years old. This is her traditional method for *fregula,* the hand-formed semolina "crumb" pasta that is unique to the island. You can make the "crumbs" small or large; small *fregula* are added to soups and the large are combined with meat or seafood in baked dishes, or used like macaroni in *pasta e fagioli* and other dishes. They can be used fresh or dried for future use.

APPROXIMATLEY ⅔ CUP COLD WATER   2 CUPS FINE SEMOLINA FLOUR

1 PACKET SAFFRON POWDER

1. Whisk together the water and the saffron.

2. Spread some of the semolina on the bottom of a large, shallow mixing bowl, preferably made of wood, and sprinkle it with enough of the water to form little "crumbs" from the moistened semolina with your hands. As you work, keep your hand rotating in the bowl, using your fingers to combine the flour and water to form the *fregula.* As the pasta "crumbs" are formed, keep adding semolina and sprinkling water until all of the semolina is used. If more water is necessary, pour some cold water into a small bowl. It is easier to dip your free hand in to sprinkle, rather than to measure out amounts of water to add to the flour. The "crumbs" should be well formed but raggy looking and not too wet. If they are too wet, add a little more semolina and work it through the *fregula.* Spread the "crumbs" out on a baking sheet, cover with clean kitchen towels, and let rest at room temperature for 20 to 30 minutes or up to 24 hours.

3. Add the *fregula* to a broth or soup like any other pasta. Or boil them in plenty of salted water for about 12 minutes; drain and toss with a smooth tomato sauce (see chapter 2).

4. To dry *fregula* for future use, preheat an oven to 200°F. Slide the sheet pan on the middle rack and bake until thoroughly dried, about 1 hour. Shake occasionally to allow for even drying. Allow to cool, then store in an airtight container for up to 1 month.

THE AUTHENTIC
SPAGHETTI ALLA CARBONARA
Serves 4

Most versions of *spaghetti alla carbonara* outside of Italy include cream, but there is no cream in the genuine recipe, which dates from World War Two. By some accounts, Italian women invented the new sauce for pasta when presented with bacon and egg rations by their American GI lovers. In any case, the sauce ingredients and method here are considered by Italian culinary historians to be the original and authentic version. While *carbonara* sauce was designed for spaghetti, I find fusilli are also a pleasant cut to use because the sauce collects nicely in its grooves.

5 EGGS, BEATEN

¾ CUP FRESHLY GRATED GRANA PADANO OR PARMIGIANO-REGGIANO CHEESE, PLUS ADDITIONAL FOR SERVING

SEA SALT AND FRESHLY GROUND BLACK PEPPER

1 POUND IMPORTED ITALIAN SPAGHETTI OR FUSILLI

2 TABLESPOONS KOSHER SALT

4 TABLESPOONS EXTRA-VIRGIN OLIVE OIL

½ POUND PANCETTA OR GUANCIALE (CHEEK BACON), THICKLY SLICED AND DICED

1. In a bowl, combine the beaten eggs with the grated cheese and season with salt and pepper.

2. Select a serving bowl for the pasta and keep it warm.

3. Fill a pot with 5 quarts water and bring it to a rapid boil over high heat. Add the spaghetti or fusilli and the kosher salt together and stir. Check the package instructions for cooking time. Cook, stirring frequently, until the pasta is 2 minutes away from being al dente.

4. Meanwhile, in a large skillet, warm the olive oil. Add the pancetta or guanciale and sauté over medium heat until nicely colored and crispy. Set aside.

5. When the pasta is ready, drain it, reserving about 1 cup of the cooking water. Transfer it to the skillet with the pancetta and toss over low heat. Add ½ cup or so of the cooking water to moisten. Simmer until the water is nearly evaporated.

6. Remove the skillet from the heat, transfer the pasta to the serving bowl, and immediately add the egg and cheese mixture, tossing vigorously to distribute the sauce while making sure it does not coagulate into scrambled egg. It should not exceed 160°F. If the pasta seems dry, add more of the reserved cooking water. Serve at once, passing the pepper mill and the grated cheese at the table.

ZIA RITA'S
CAPPELLINI WITH TOMATO AND PANCETTA
Serves 4

My aunt Rita grew up in a convent in Cagliari during the war when food was hard to come by even on the pastoral island of Sardinia. But the nuns made whatever provisions they did have taste good by using local aromatics skillfully. Whether my aunt picked up that gift for simple but artful cooking from the good sisters, or whether she inherited her instincts from her father, a legendary connoisseur of good food and wine, her flare for elevating simple ingredients is evident in this zesty, quick, and easy pasta dish, which can be assembled and cooked in less than half an hour. If using bacon in place of pancetta, blanch it for 1 minute before chopping. The hot pepper adds a nice pep.

2 TABLESPOONS EXTRA-VIRGIN OLIVE OIL	1 28-OUNCE CAN ITALIAN PLUM TOMATOES, CRUSHED
½ POUND PANCETTA OR BLANCHED BACON, CHOPPED	SEA SALT
1 ONION, CHOPPED	1 POUND IMPORTED ITALIAN CAPPELLINI
2 LARGE CLOVES GARLIC, SMASHED	2 TABLESPOONS KOSHER SALT
10 TO 20 HOT RED PEPPERS, SEEDED AND CHOPPED	FRESHLY GRATED PECORINO CHEESE, FOR SERVING

1. In a large skillet, warm the olive oil over medium-low heat. Add the pancetta or bacon, onion, garlic, and hot peppers. Sauté until the mixture is lightly colored and aromatic, about 10 minutes. Drain off some but not all of the excess fat, as it adds terrific flavor to the sauce. Stir in the tomatoes and salt to taste.

2. In the meantime, in a pot, bring 5 quarts water to a rapid boil over high heat. Add the pasta and kosher salt all at once and stir. Consult the cooking time on the pasta box and cook over high heat, stirring frequently, until the pasta is 3 minutes short of done. Drain, reserving 1 cup or so of the pasta water should you need it later.

3. Transfer the cappellini to the skillet with the sauce and cook over medium heat, tossing frequently, for 2 minutes, or until the pasta is al dente. If necessary, add some of the reserved pasta water to moisten. Serve at once, passing the grated cheese at the table.

CAPPELLINI AGLIO E OLIO
Serves 4

Another of my aunt's triumphs in simple cooking. Because cappellini are very fine, they can overcook all too easily. *Fidellini,* which are a slightly thicker than *cappellini,* work even better here, but they aren't as easy to find in our supermarkets. This departure from the usual way of cooking them works very well. This dish is terrific on its own, or it makes a happy union with many meat or poultry dishes.

½ TEASPOON RED PEPPER FLAKES

¾ CUP EXTRA-VIRGIN OLIVE OIL

12 LARGE CLOVES GARLIC, CHOPPED

SEA SALT

1 POUND IMPORTED ITALIAN CAPPELLINI OR FIDELLINI

2 TABLESPOONS KOSHER SALT

1 CUP FRESH BASIL, CUT INTO JULIENNE

1. Warm the red pepper flakes n a large skillet over medium-low heat. Add the olive oil and warm. Add the garlic. Sauté until the garlic is an even golden color. Turn off the heat at once.

2. When you are ready to eat, in a pot bring 5 quarts water to a rapid boil over high heat. Add the pasta and kosher salt all at once and stir. Cover and turn off the heat. Allow to rest until the pasta is al dente. Drain, reserving 1 cup or so of the pasta water should you need it later.

3. Transfer the *cappellini* to the skillet, add the basil, and toss all together. If necessary, add some of the reserved pasta cooking water to moisten. Serve at once.

SPAGHETTI with SAUTÉED RADICCHIO

Serves 2 to 4

I corresponded with Paolo Lanapoppi, a Venetian writer and gondola restorer, for some time before I finally tracked him down in Venice. When we finally met, the radicchio of nearby Treviso was in full flower, and he cooked up this delightful homespun dish for lunch over talk of *carnevale* and gondolas. Paolo topped the pasta generously with Parmigiano-Reggiano cheese at the table, but it is equally delicious without the cheese.

6 TABLESPOONS EXTRA-VIRGIN OLIVE OIL

1 RED ONION, THINLY SLICED AND THEN CHOPPED

8 TO 10 OUNCES RADICCHIO, PREFERABLY THE ELONGATED TARDIVO VARIETY, CUT INTO JULIENNE AND THEN ROUGHLY CHOPPED

½ CUP HOT WATER

½ TEASPOON SEA SALT, OR TO TASTE

¾ POUND IMPORTED ITALIAN SPAGHETTI

2 TABLESPOONS KOSHER SALT

FRESHLY GROUND BLACK PEPPER

FRESHLY GRATED PARMIGIANO-REGGIANO CHEESE, FOR SERVING

1. In an ample skillet, warm the olive oil over medium-low heat. Add the onion and sauté until nicely softened and lightly colored, about 6 minutes. Toss in the radicchio, and use a wooden spoon to coat it evenly in the olive oil. Add the water, continuing to toss. Cover and continue to cook over medium-low heat, stirring occasionally, until the radicchio is tender, 10 to 12 minutes. Add the sea salt, cover, and set aside.

2. Bring a large pot filled with water over high heat to a rolling boil. Stir in the pasta and kosher salt. Cook, always over the highest heat possible and stirring constantly to prevent the pasta strands from sticking together, until the spaghetti is almost cooked, about 6 minutes. Add a glass of cold water to the pot to arrest the boiling and drain immediately, setting aside about 1 cup of the cooking water. Add the spaghetti to the skillet, and return the heat to high. Use 2 long forks to distribute all the ingredients evenly, about 1 minute. If necessary, add a little of the pasta water to moisten so that everything mixes nicely together. Serve immediately with plenty of pepper and pass the Parmigiano-Reggiano cheese at the table.

SPAGHETTI with CLAM SAUCE,
RED VERSION

Serves 4

Is there any dish more reminiscent than this one of the proverbial Italian repast eaten by moonlight at some romantic seaside spot—say, Amalfi or Sorrento? It was not until I took my first trip to southern Italy as a young woman that I knew what this dish should really taste like, and perhaps it was the grip of romance that made it so indescribably beguiling. But even in my American kitchen, there is a certain magic in it, and I cook it regularly. Note that grated cheese should never be added to seafood sauces for pasta.

⅓ CUP SEA SALT, PLUS MORE FOR SEASONING

1 CUP CORNMEAL

4 POUNDS COCKLES OR MANILA CLAMS, OR 4 DOZEN SMALL LITTLENECK CLAMS

⅓ CUP EXTRA-VIRGIN OLIVE OIL

6 LARGE CLOVES GARLIC, CRUSHED

4 TABLESPOONS CHOPPED FRESH FLAT-LEAF PARSLEY

3 LARGE RIPE TOMATOES, PEELED, SEEDED, AND CHOPPED, OR 1 CUP CANNED PLUM TOMATOES, DRAINED, SEEDED, AND CHOPPED

½ CUP CLAM JUICE OR GOOD-QUALITY DRY WHITE WINE

FRESHLY GROUND BLACK PEPPER

2 TABLESPOONS KOSHER SALT

1 POUND SPAGHETTI OR THIN LINGUINE

CRUSTY ARTISAN BREAD, FOR SERVING

1. Mix the salt and cornmeal in 1 gallon water and soak the clams for 3 to 4 hours so that they purge themselves of sand or other matter. (Make sure you use sea or kosher salt, as the iodine in regular salt will kill the clams before they hit the boiling water.) One hour before cooking, scrub the clams well with a stiff vegetable brush under cold running water and rinse them until they are free of sand. Before cooking, tap any open clams. If they close, keep them; if not, discard at once.

2. In a large skillet over medium-low heat, warm the olive oil. Add the garlic and parsley, and cook until the garlic is lightly colored, about 5 minutes. Add the tomatoes and allow to simmer over medium heat for 2 to 3 minutes. Add the clam juice or wine and simmer gently for 3 to 4 minutes. Add the scrubbed clams, cover tightly, and steam over medium heat until the clams open. Add sea salt and pepper to taste. Lift out any empty shells, and discard any clams that did not open. You can use the sauce with the clams in their shells or, if preferred, shell some of the clams and leave the remainder in their shells for effect. (It's fun to suck the tasty clams out of their shells, digging in with your hands, as the Italians do.)

3. While the clams are cooking, in a pot, bring 5 quarts water to a rapid boil over high heat. Add the 2 tablespoons kosher salt and the pasta. Stir immediately and continue to stir occasionally to prevent the strands from sticking together. Cook for 1 minute less than indicated on the package directions for al dente. Drain well and immediately add the pasta to the clam sauce in the skillet and toss. Serve immediately and pass the bread at the table for soaking up the sauce—not a drop should go to waste!

LINGUINE WITH TUNA SAUCE AND PARSLEY

Serves 4 to 6

This sauce might be overlooked because it is made with canned tuna, but premium Italian tuna cut from the belly of the fish is pink, tender, and sweet, and it dissolves easily into a delicious and quick sauce for pasta. White albacore tuna or tuna packed in its own juices or in spring water won't do; they are just too dry for this sauce.

5 TABLESPOONS EXTRA-VIRGIN OLIVE OIL

4 LARGE CLOVES GARLIC, SMASHED

1 TEASPOON MINCED FRESH THYME

5 TABLESPOONS CHOPPED FRESH
FLAT-LEAF PARSLEY

7-OUNCE CAN PREMIUM ITALIAN TUNA
PACKED IN OLIVE OIL, DRAINED AND
FINELY CHOPPED

½ CUP GOOD-QUALITY DRY WHITE WINE

PINCH OF RED PEPPER FLAKES

1 POUND IMPORTED ITALIAN THIN
LINGUINE

2 TABLESPOONS KOSHER SALT

1. In a large skillet, warm the oil. Add the garlic and sauté over medium-low heat until it is soft and fragrant, about 2 minutes. Stir in the thyme, half the parsley, and the chopped tuna. Add the wine to the pan to form a sauce. Add the pepper flakes and simmer for 5 minutes over medium-low heat. Add the remaining parsley.

2. Bring 5 quarts water in a pot to a rapid boil over high heat. Add the pasta and the kosher salt to the boiling water and cook according to package instructions over high heat, stirring. When it is cooked 1 minute less than al dente, drain, reserving ½ cup of the cooking water.

3. Transfer the pasta to the skillet with the tuna sauce and toss all together. If necessary, add a few tablespoons of the pasta water to add moisture. Serve at once.

MACARONI with BROCCOLI SAUCE
Serves 4

This rustic dish is a specialty of Puglia, a part of southern Italy from which many immigrants came—my own paternal grandparents included. It never ceases to evoke in me a renewed awe for real, exuberant southern Italian food of the sort most Americans rarely experience. My sisters and I loved this pasta so much that we fought for it if any was left at the bottom of the bowl—even after we had had second helpings. My mother eventually learned to make double what she usually made, and the next day for lunch, she warmed up the leftovers in a frying pan until it was hot and crisp—and we fought over that, too! Don't be put off by the anchovies in the sauce; they dissolve completely into the hot olive oil to form the sauce. Even avowed anchovy haters for whom I have made this dish have loved it. Note: Don't add grated cheese, please.

1 LARGE HEAD BROCCOLI

2 TABLESPOONS KOSHER SALT

1 POUND RIGATONI, ZITI, PENNE, OR PENNE RIGATE

½ CUP EXTRA-VIRGIN OLIVE OIL

1½ CANS ANCHOVY FILLETS PRESERVED IN OLIVE OIL

1. Wash and trim the broccoli, cutting off any tough or discolored parts. Divide the top part into florets, and slice the stalks into 2-inch pieces.

2. In an ample pot, bring 7 quarts water to a rapid boil. Stir in the salt, the broccoli, and the pasta all at once. Cook over high heat until the pasta is al dente and the broccoli is soft and creamy. Stir several times as the pasta cooks to prevent it from sticking together and to allow even cooking.

3. Meanwhile, in a large skillet, warm the olive oil and the anchovies together, including the oil from one of the anchovy cans. The anchovies will dissolve completely in the oil, forming the basis of the sauce. Keep warm.

4. When the pasta is cooked, drain it, but don't over-drain; it should still be moist and dripping a little. Toss the pasta and broccoli with the anchovy sauce in the skillet. Serve immediately.

PUGLIA-STYLE SHORT PASTA
WITH COOL SUMMER SAUCE

Serves 4 to 6

Another dish from my father's native region that I learned from my Italian friend Anna Maria Erenbourg Weld. Anna Maria often spends her summers at her brother's home in Otranto, an ancient port on the tip of Puglia's western coastline. The best gifts she brings back are robust recipes, like this one, which she learned from a local woman who grows vegetables in her courtyard and likes to share cooking advice with her neighbors.

EXTRA-VIRGIN OLIVE OIL FOR GREASING, PLUS ½ CUP FOR THE SAUCE

SEA SALT

½ TEASPOON DRIED OREGANO

2 PINTS SWEET VINE-RIPENED CHERRY TOMATOES, HALVED

¼ POUND IMPORTED SMOKED OR UNSMOKED RICOTTA SALATA, OR SUBSTITUTE FETA, CRUMBLED

2 TABLESPOONS CHOPPED FRESH MINT

1 SMALL DRIED HOT RED PEPPER, SEEDS REMOVED, MINCED, OR SUBSTITUTE ½ TEASPOON RED PEPPER FLAKES

1 POUND IMPORTED ITALIAN SHORT PASTA SUCH AS PENNE OR MEDIUM-SIZE RIGATONI

2 TABLESPOONS KOSHER SALT

1. Preheat an oven to 425°F.

2. Grease a baking sheet with olive oil. Sprinkle lightly with sea salt and scatter the oregano. Place the cherry tomatoes, cut side down, on the pan. Slide the pan on the middle rack of the oven and bake until a liquid forms on the bottom of the pan, but no more than 10 minutes; the tomatoes should not actually cook. Reserve the tomato juices.

3. In a serving bowl, combine the ½ cup olive oil, baked tomatoes, cheese, mint, red pepper, and sea salt to taste.

4. In the meantime, bring 5 quarts water in a pot to a rapid boil over high heat. Add the pasta and kosher salt at the same time and stir. Consult the cooking directions on the back of the pasta box and continue to cook over high heat, stirring frequently, until the pasta is cooked al dente. Drain, transfer the pasta to the serving bowl, and toss with the sauce and the reserved tomato juices. Serve at once.

STEWED LENTILS
WITH SAGE
Serves 3 to 4

Here is a popular dish that is eaten both as a meatless side dish and as a main course with roasted pork sausages. Boiling the lentils before cooking them in the sauce sweetens them naturally. For centuries, lentils have been a food of the poor, who couldn't afford the luxury of buying meat. As a result, Italian housewives have made lentil cookery into an art, such as this rib-sticking and nutritious dish infused with the flavors of a rich vegetable *battuto,* garlic, and sage.

2 CUPS DRIED BROWN LENTILS

1 BAY LEAF

3 TEASPOONS SEA SALT, PLUS MORE TO TASTE

½ CUP EXTRA-VIRGIN OLIVE OIL, PLUS MORE FOR DRIZZLING

2 CARROTS, MINCED

1 TENDER CELERY HEART WITH LEAVES, MINCED

1 LARGE ONION, MINCED

6 LARGE CLOVES GARLIC, SMASHED

1 8-INCH SAGE SPRIG

2 CUPS 20-MINUTE TOMATO SAUCE (PAGE 37) OR CANNED TOMATO SAUCE

1. Rinse and pick over the lentils; drain. Put the lentils and bay leaf in a pot and add cold water to cover by 3 inches. Bring to a boil. Reduce the heat to a simmer and cook until not quite tender, about 20 minutes. Skim off any foam that forms at the top. Turn off the heat, stir in the salt, and let stand for 5 to 10 minutes. Drain and set aside, reserving the cooking liquid. Discard the bay leaf.

2. In a large skillet, warm the ½ cup olive oil and add the carrots, celery, onion, garlic, and sage. Sauté, stirring occasionally, until softened, about 10 minutes. Stir in the drained lentils. Add salt to taste and the tomato sauce and enough lentil cooking liquid to cover, about ½ cup, or as needed. Cover, reduce the heat to low, and simmer, stirring occasionally, until the lentils are tender, about 10 minutes. Add more lentil water as necessary to keep the lentils from drying out; the consistency of the stew should be loose but not watery.

3. Turn off the heat and let stand for about 10 minutes. Taste for salt, fish out the sage, and serve. Drizzle a little extra-virgin olive oil over each serving for added flavor.

SIMMERED WHITE BEANS
WITH SAUSAGE AND TOMATO

A side dish for 4

When I was growing up, my mother often reminisced about the things she missed from her native Italy. The flavor of Italian beans was one of them. I have friends who carry beans back from Tuscany—the home of true bean lovers—when they go there because Tuscan beans are so flavorful. In this dish, the sauce and succulent fennel sausages give great flavor to the beans, which become saturated with their juices.

2 TABLESPOONS EXTRA-VIRGIN OLIVE OIL

1 ONION, FINELY CHOPPED

2 CLOVES GARLIC, FINELY CHOPPED

3 SWEET ITALIAN FENNEL SAUSAGES (ABOUT ½ POUND TOTAL WEIGHT), CASINGS REMOVED

1 TABLESPOON TOMATO PASTE

3 CHOPPED FRESH SAGE LEAVES OR ½ TEASPOON DRIED SAGE

½ CUP TASTY MEAT BROTH (PAGE XX), OR WATER

½ TEASPOON SALT, OR TO TASTE

FRESHLY GROUND BLACK PEPPER

1½ CUPS COOKED, DRAINED CANNELLINI OR GREAT NORTHERN BEANS (PAGE 213)

1 TABLESPOON CHOPPED FRESH FLAT-LEAF PARSLEY

1. In a skillet over medium-low heat, warm the olive oil. Add the onion and garlic and sauté gently until totally softened but not browned, about 5 minutes. Using a slotted spoon, remove the onion and garlic from the pan and transfer to a side dish.

2. Heat the oil that remains in the pan and add the sausage meat to it, breaking it up with a wooden spoon. Sauté until browned, stirring occasionally, about 5 minutes. Return the onion and garlic to the pan. Add the tomato paste, sage, broth or water, salt, and pepper to taste and bring to a boil. Add the beans, bring to a boil again, and immediately reduce to a simmer. Partially cover and cook gently for 10 to 15 minutes. Sprinkle with the parsley and serve hot or warm.

NONNA GIULIA'S
POLENTA LAYER CAKE WITH MEAT SAUCE

Serves 8

My maternal grandmother's polenta cake is much like baked lasagne except that polenta replaces pasta in between layers of winey meat sauce and tangy young sheep's-milk cheese. Nonna Giulia died long before I was born, but her recipe for this provincial Sardinian dish, called *pasticciata di polenta* in Italian, was one of her jewels, and passed down by my mother.

FOR THE SAUCE

6 TABLESPOONS EXTRA-VIRGIN OLIVE OIL

1 ONION, MINCED

1 CARROT, CHOPPED

1 SMALL CELERY STALK WITH LEAVES, CHOPPED

1 TEASPOON GROUND FENNEL SEEDS

1 POUND GROUND LEAN PORK, OR MIXED GROUND PORK AND BEEF

½ CUP GOOD-QUALITY DRY RED WINE

3 TABLESPOONS TOMATO PASTE

1 35-OUNCE CAN PLUM TOMATOES, DRAINED, SEEDED, AND CHOPPED, JUICES RESERVED

3 TABLESPOONS MINCED BASIL LEAVES

1 TEASPOON SEA SALT

1 RECIPE BASIC POLENTA, PAGE 217

½ POUND SEMISOFT *PECORINO* CHEESE SUCH AS *FIOR DI SARDEGNA*, OR TUSCAN *CACIOTTA*, OR SUBSTITUTE SPANISH *MANCHEGO*, SHREDDED

OLIVE OR VEGETABLE OIL, FOR OILING POLENTA BOARD OR WORK SURFACE

1. To make the sauce, warm the oil in a skillet. Stir in the onion, carrot, and celery and continue to sauté until soft, 10 minutes. Add the fennel seeds and pork and sauté over low heat until the meat colors lightly, stirring occasionally, about 4 minutes. Stir in the wine and allow to evaporate, 1 minute. Add the tomato paste diluted in some of the reserved tomato juices followed by the tomatoes, another ½ cup tomato juices, basil, and the salt. Stir well. Partially cover and simmer over the lowest heat for 1 hour, stirring frequently, until the sauce is thick and fragrant. Add more tomato juices during cooking if the sauce seems to be drying out.

2. Lightly oil a 9 x 13-inch baking dish and set aside. Make the polenta and turn it out onto a lightly oiled board or counter surface. Use a rubber spatula or knife dipped into hot water to spread it out into a rectangle about ¼ inch thick. Let stand until cooled completely and firm, about 15 minutes. Cut into 3-inch squares; set aside.

3. Heat an oven to 450°F. Arrange half the polenta squares in the bottom of the baking dish. Pour half the sauce over the polenta squares and spread to cover. Sprinkle half the cheese over the sauce. Repeat with another layer of each. Bake until the "cake" is heated through and the cheese is golden brown, between 15 and 20 minutes. Let stand for 10 minutes. Cut into portions and serve.

STEAMING POLENTA
WITH TALEGGIO CHEESE

Serves 4

I was first served this homey dish in Lombardy, land of sublime taleggio cheese. Taleggio and polenta is a logical marriage in this polenta-eating, cheese-producing part of Italy, and now it is standard fare in my kitchen as well. There is nothing to it: Pour steaming polenta directly from the cooking pot onto a large platter and top with hunks of this rich, buttery cheese. A few pointers: Be sure to add the polenta to the water in a slow, steady trickle, stirring all the while, to prevent lumps from forming. While I prefer unprocessed, long-cooking polenta for its creaminess and superior flavor, it is hard to find in America. Substitute a Spanish brand of polenta cornmeal or organic polenta meal rather than instant polenta, which is far more pricey and not as good. Polenta should be made in time to serve it immediately, from pot to table.

4 TABLESPOONS UNSALTED BUTTER, MELTED

1½ POUNDS IMPORTED ITALIAN TALEGGIO CHEESE, AT ROOM TEMPERATURE

2 QUARTS WATER

2 TABLESPOONS COARSE SALT

3 CUPS COARSE POLENTA CORNMEAL

ADDITIONAL BOILING WATER, IF NECESSARY

1. Drizzle the melted butter in an ample wide and shallow serving dish. Cut the crust off the taleggio and have it ready to spoon over the polenta after it is cooked.

2. Fill a deep, heavy pot with the 2 quarts water and bring it to a rolling boil over high heat. Add the salt, and little by little, pour in the cornmeal, using a sturdy wooden spoon or whisk to stir well and continuously. Cook over medium heat, stirring the polenta often; this is important if the polenta is to become properly soft and creamy. The polenta is ready when it is so thick that it begins to resist stirring and pulls away easily from the sides of the pan with the spoon or whisk (40 to 50 minutes or more for unprocessed polenta; about 20 minutes for Spanish or organic polenta). If the polenta is quite thick but still not pulling away easily from the pan, add a little more boiling water and continue to stir until it is ready.

3. Pour the polenta, piping hot, into the serving dish. Spoon the taleggio, which by now has softened, on top of the polenta. Use a large serving spoon to dish the polenta and cheese onto individual plates and serve at once.

BREAD PASTICCIO

Serves 4 to 6

In Italy, this is called *lasagne povera,* or "poor lasagne," because leftover bread is used in place of pasta. Make it in the summer when you can get fresh, sweet vine-ripened tomatoes in season. It makes a scrumptious snack or a memorable side dish.

EXTRA-VIRGIN OLIVE OIL, FOR GREASING

¾ POUND STALE BREAD, STILL SOFT ENOUGH TO CUT, CRUSTS REMOVED, THINLY SLICED

1 QUART TASTY MEAT BROTH (PAGE 213) OR VEGETABLE BROTH (PAGE 215)

1½ POUNDS SWEET, JUICY VINE-RIPENED TOMATOES, PEELED AND ROUGHLY CHOPPED

10 FRESH BASIL LEAVES, MINCED

2 TEASPOONS MINCED FRESH MARJORAM OR THYME, OR 1 TEASPOON DRIED

½ POUND MOZZARELLA, SHREDDED

¼ CUP FRESHLY GRATED PARMIGIANO-REGGIANO OR GRANA PADANO

4 LARGE EGGS

¼ CUP MILK

½ TEASPOON SALT

1. Preheat an oven to 325°F. Select a 9 x 12-inch or equivalent baking dish (preferably nonstick) with high sides, and brush it generously with extra-virgin olive oil.

2. Soak half the bread in the broth until it has absorbed as much liquid as it can without falling apart. Arrange the slices on the bottom of the prepared baking dish. Over that, arrange a layer of the tomatoes, then scatter half of the basil and thyme. Follow with a layer of mozzarella, followed by a scattering of half the grated cheese. Soak the remaining bread and repeat the layers with the remaining ingredients.

3. Beat the eggs with the milk and the salt and pour over all. Poke holes through the top to enable the egg to penetrate the lower layer. Grease well the shiny side of a piece of foil large enough to cover the dish; cover tightly. Slide the baking dish onto the center rack of the oven and cook for 1 hour. Remove the foil and bake for another 10 minutes to allow the top to color nicely.

4. Remove the baking dish from the oven and allow to settle for 10 to 20 minutes. Use a metal spatula to dislodge the "lasagne" from the sides of the pan. Cut into individual portions and serve hot or warm.

CHAPTER

6

MAIN DISHES:
POULTRY

When I was young my Italian relatives always talked about how chickens used to taste. No wonder. The birds then roamed freely around the farm, pecking and scratching for food as the Lord intended, and were slaughtered only hours before cooking. Modern, mass-produced chickens—what my mother used to call "factory-made"—have ruled the roost in the U.S. for decades and will continue to do so, but organic, free-range, or naturally raised poultry is becoming readily available, even in supermarkets. Italians prefer their chicken on the bone (where the flavor is best), as in *pollo alla cacciatore,* and turkey, once uncommon, has become more popular. Both birds are bred small and tender in Italy, unlike the larger and less tender American ones. Note that breast meat is comparatively bland and dries out easily. The dark meat is moister and more flavorful and, for the most part, the one that I include in these recipes.

ZIA ANNA'S
ROASTED CHICKEN WITH SAFFRON STUFFING
Serves 4

This beguiling recipe with its Sardinian flavors and hint of saffron transforms ordinary roast chicken into a feast. The golden-tinted, aromatic stuffing can be used for all types of fowl, including guinea hen or turkey. If you have the giblets, liver, and wattles of the bird, include them in the stuffing for added flavor. Use plain artisanal bread with no added flavorings.

4½-POUND FREE-RANGE CHICKEN AT ROOM TEMPERATURE, INCLUDING LIVER AND GIBLETS, IF AVAILABLE	3 SWEET ITALIAN PORK SAUSAGES FLAVORED WITH FENNEL, CASINGS REMOVED
SEA SALT AND FRESHLY GROUND BLACK PEPPER	5 TABLESPOONS FRESH CHOPPED FLAT-LEAF PARSLEY
1 LARGE ONION, QUARTERED	5 FRESH BASIL LEAVES, CHOPPED
3 TABLESPOONS EXTRA-VIRGIN OLIVE OIL, PLUS MORE FOR RUBBING INTO BIRD	8 SUN-DRIED TOMATO HALVES, RECONSTITUTED AND CHOPPED
2 TABLESPOONS UNSALTED BUTTER, PLUS MORE FOR FINISHING STUFFING	6 CUPS DICED PACKED, DAY-OLD BREAD, CRUSTS REMOVED
1 ONION, CHOPPED	¼ HEAPING TEASPOON SAFFRON THREADS, OR 2 ENVELOPES PURE SAFFRON POWDER
2 MEDIUM CELERY STALKS, INCLUDING LEAVES, CHOPPED	1½ CUPS CHICKEN BROTH (PAGE 214), OR MORE IF NEEDED

1. Preheat an oven to 450°F. Wash the chicken in cold water and dry thoroughly, inside and out. Sprinkle the cavity with salt and pepper and stuff with the quartered onion; fasten closed with toothpicks and truss the bird, keeping the wings and legs close to the body. If using giblets, wash and dry them. Discard the whitish membrane on the gizzard and chop coarse. Set the bird aside at room temperature.

2. In an ample skillet, warm the olive oil and butter over medium heat and add the onion and celery. Sauté for about 8 minutes, stirring occasionally. Add the giblets and sausage and sauté gently, stirring occasionally, until browned and cooked through, another 8 minutes. Add the parsley, basil, and sun-dried tomatoes. Sauté until soft. Stir in the bread and sauté for another few minutes to coat it.

3. Dissolve the saffron powder in 1 cup of the broth. Pour it over the bread in the skillet and combine thoroughly. Season with salt and pepper. Taste to ensure that the stuffing is moist. If it is too dry, add up to another ½ cup broth. Transfer to a buttered medium baking dish. Dot the surface with butter, cover with buttered foil, and refrigerate until ready to bake.

4. Place the chicken on a rack in a roasting pan just the right size. Rub the skin lightly with olive oil. Sprinkle 2 teaspoons salt on the surface of the bird for a nice uniform coating and crisp, flavorful skin. Place the bird breast side down. Pour ¼ inch broth in the bottom of the roasting pan.

5. Reduce the oven temperature to 375°F and set the chicken on the middle rack. Roast the chicken for 30 minutes. Remove and breast side up. Roast for another 30 minutes. Turn breast side down for the last stretch. Baste each time you take the chicken out of the oven to turn it. In total, roast the bird 20 minutes per pound, or until a thermometer slipped into the thigh registers 165°F, or the juices run clear when pierced. About 15 minutes before the chicken is finished, slide the stuffing on the rack next to the bird and cook for 20 to 25 minutes, removing the foil during the last 5 minutes to form a golden crust.

6. Remove the chicken from the oven, tent with foil, and allow to settle for 15 minutes. De-fat the pan juices to pass at the table. Remove the string on the bird, carve, and sprinkle with pepper. Serve, spooning some of the stuffing onto each dish.

WHOLE ROASTED CHICKEN
WITH GARLIC, FRESH GARDEN HERBS, AND PAN GRAVY

Serves 4

My first lesson in procuring chicken took place as a girl on a trip to the Cagliari market with my aunt Anna. She went from stall to stall, asking the meat purveyors if their chicken was "machine-made" or not. If it wasn't raised in a barnyard, pecking and scratching for grubs and grasses, she wouldn't have any part of it. Here was one of her methods for roasting those succulent free-range chickens, which is easily done in a home oven or outdoors on a spit.

4½-POUND FREE-RANGE ROASTING HEN, AT ROOM TEMPERATURE

2 TEASPOONS FENNEL SEEDS, GROUND

HANDFUL OF FRESH THYME, TWIGS AND LEAVES

LARGE PINCH OF CAYENNE PEPPER

12 CLOVES GARLIC, SMASHED

SEA SALT

HANDFUL OF FRESH SAGE, TWIGS AND LEAVES

HANDFUL OF FRESH ROSEMARY, TWIGS AND LEAVES

2 CUPS CHICKEN BROTH (PAGE 214)

⅓ CUP GOOD-QUALITY DRY WHITE WINE

1. Preheat an oven to 425°F. Remove excess fat from the chicken. Wash it inside and out under cold running water and use strong paper towels to pat it thoroughly dry.

2. In a small bowl, mix the fennel, thyme, and cayenne pepper. Rub the inside of the cavity with one garlic clove and half the spice mixture. Sprinkle with salt. Place all the garlic and most of the herbs inside, reserving some for garnish. Rub the outside of the bird with the remaining spice mixture, loosely tie the legs together, and place breast side up in a roasting pan. Pour the broth to reach ¼ inch up the sides.

3. Roast for 30 minutes. Reduce the heat to 400°F, then turn the bird breast side down for another 30 minutes. Baste every 15 minutes with pan juices, adding more broth as it evaporates. Turn breast side up and roast until done, another 20 minutes, or until an instant-read meat thermometer reads 165°F. Transfer to a carving board and cover loosely with foil. Let rest for 20 to 30 minutes before carving.

4. To make the gravy, pour the pan juices through a fine mesh strainer. Transfer it to a fat separator and set aside. Warm the roasting pan over over medium heat. Add the wine and use a wooden spoon to dislodge any bits stuck to the bottom of the pan. Simmer for 2 minutes. Strain the liquid into the fat separator as well.

5. Carve the bird and arrange nicely on a warm platter. Discard the herbs from the cavity. Add juices that have collected during carving to the gravy you have made. Garnish with the reserved fresh herbs and serve at once.

ANNA AMENDOLARA'S
BAKED CHICKEN WITH TOMATOES AND GARLIC

Serves 4

Anna Amendolara Nurse is a beloved mentor to culinary stars and students alike—or anyone else who comes her way and wants to learn about Italian cooking. I especially love her homey southern Italian dishes because they hark back to the food of my own paternal ancestors, who came from the same town in Puglia as Anna's parents. This exceptional yet easy dish cries for fresh summer vine-ripened tomatoes, but imported canned Italian plum tomatoes can be substituted successfully. This dish creates profuse pan juices, so plan on having plenty of good artisan bread on hand, or toss the juices with a half pound of freshly cooked pasta. Alternatively, serve the chicken as a main course with salad and reserve the extra pan juices for fortifying another sauce or a soup.

3½-POUND WHOLE FREE-RANGE CHICKEN

8 FRESH VINE-RIPENED PLUM TOMATOES, OR 8 DRAINED IMPORTED ITALIAN PLUM TOMATOES

3 LARGE CLOVES GARLIC, SLICED

⅓ COARSELY CHOPPED FRESH FLAT-LEAF PARSLEY

⅓ CUP EXTRA-VIRGIN OLIVE OIL

SEA SALT AND FRESHLY GROUND BLACK PEPPER

1. Preheat an oven to 400°F. Wash and dry the chicken. Cut through the breast to open the chicken like a book.

2. Cut off the stem end of the tomatoes. With your hands, break open each tomato and squeeze out excess seeds and juice. Scatter half the tomatoes on the bottom of a roasting pan large enough to accommodate the chicken. Lay the chicken, skin side down, over the tomatoes. Scatter the remaining tomatoes, the garlic, and parsley on top of the chicken, drizzle with olive oil, and season with salt and pepper. Add ½ cup water to the pan.

3. Bake until the chicken is lightly browned on top, about 30 minutes. Turn the chicken over, rearranging the tomatoes and garlic on top. Bake until the chicken skin is nicely browned, about 30 to 40 minutes, or until an instant-read meat thermometer inserted into the thickest part of the thigh away from the bone registers 165°F. Add a little more water if the pan juices seem to be drying up; no more than a tablespoon or two, if any, should be necessary. Baste the chicken occasionally as it bakes to keep the breast meat moist. Remove the chicken from the oven and allow to settle for 15 minutes before carving. Serve hot.

CHICKEN CUTLETS WITH CRUNCHY COATING
AND ARUGULA AND TOMATO TOPPING

Serves 4

Italians prefer chicken on the bone to comparatively bland-tasting breast meat, but creating a crunchy bread coating and adding a topping of arugula and sweet tomatoes transforms dry cutlets into a succulent dish. Turkey breast cutlets or veal cutlets can be used interchangeably with chicken breasts for this easy but elegant dish.

FOR THE SAUCE

¼ CUP EXTRA-VIRGIN OLIVE OIL

¼ TEASPOON SALT, OR TO TASTE

FRESHLY GROUND BLACK PEPPER

1 POUND FRESH, SWEET, MATURE VINE-RIPENED TOMATOES

1 SMALL BUNCH ARUGULA (TO YIELD 1 CUP PACKED LEAVES)

2 TABLESPOONS MINCED VIDALIA OR RED ONION

2 WHOLE CHICKEN BREASTS, DE-BONED AND PARTIALLY FROZEN

2 LARGE EGGS, BEATEN

1 TABLESPOON GRATED ONION

SEA SALT AND FRESHLY GROUND BLACK PEPPER

1½ CUPS LIGHTLY TOASTED PANKO CRUMBS OR WHITE BREAD CRUMBS

6 TABLESPOONS EXTRA-VIRGIN OLIVE OIL, OR AS NEEDED

1. To make the sauce, combine the olive oil, salt, and pepper to taste in a serving bowl. Cut out each tomato core and cut the tomatoes in half lengthwise. Push out the excess seeds, chop the tomatoes coarse, and add to the bowl.

2. Wash the arugula under cold running water then drain. Remove the stems and yellow leaves and dry thoroughly. Chop coarse and add it and the onion to the sauce. Toss well and leave at room temperature for 30 minutes to 2 hours.

3. Put the chicken breasts on a cutting board and separate them where they naturally divide down the middle. Using a very sharp knife, slice each breast section laterally into 3 slices to make very thin, even cutlets. Beat together the eggs, grated onion, salt, and pepper. Spread the panko or bread crumbs on a piece of wax paper.

4. Heat the oil in a sauté pan until it is hot enough for the chicken to sizzle. Just before frying, dip each cutlet into the egg mixture to coat on both sides, then into the crumbs, patting each to cover completely. Sauté the breasts over medium heat until they are golden on the outside but still tender and moist within, 2 to 3 minutes on each side. Drain on paper towels. Bread the second batch of cutlets just before slipping them into the pan. Repeat the frying and draining procedure.

5. Transfer to serving plates and spoon sauce on top. Pass more sauce at the table.

PEPPERY FRIED CHICKEN WINGS
WITH GARLIC AND ROSEMARY

Serves 4

This is one of my favorite ways of making chicken wings, adapted from a recipe for fried chicken that I learned to make from a Tuscan woman I knew. The chicken becomes crispy outside and aromatic and succulent inside, with a terrific little kick from the cayenne pepper. If you like it hot, add more cayenne pepper.

16 CHICKEN WINGS, AT ROOM TEMPERATURE

8 LARGE CLOVES GARLIC, MINCED

4 TABLESPOONS MINCED FRESH ROSEMARY, OR 2 TABLESPOONS CRUSHED DRIED ROSEMARY

1½ CUPS UNBLEACHED FLOUR

SEA SALT

¼ TEASPOON CAYENNE PEPPER

3 LARGE EGGS

GRAPE SEED, SAFFLOWER, OR OTHER VEGETABLE OIL, FOR FRYING

1. Wash the wings and pat dry thoroughly with paper towels. Keep the wing tips intact and cut the wings at the joint to separate the drummettes. In a bowl, combine the wings with the garlic and rosemary, and massage the herbs into the meat.

2. Spread the flour on a sheet of wax paper. Season with salt and plenty of cayenne pepper. Beat the eggs in a wide bowl next to the wax paper. Place a large platter, lined with a double layer of paper towels, and additional paper towels, nearby.

3. Pour the oil to a depth of about 1 inch in a large, heavy-bottomed skillet and warm over medium heat until sizzling hot. Just before you are ready to begin frying, lightly dredge each piece of wing in the flour. Dip the wing piece into the beaten eggs to coat, then dredge lightly in the flour once again. (Keep in mind that if the chicken is coated in flour and egg and left to sit for even a few minutes, the coating will become soggy and the chicken will not be crisp and light.)

4. Slip the chicken wing pieces into the hot oil, piece by piece. Do not crowd the pan with too many pieces at once, or they will not cook evenly. Fry until golden and thoroughly cooked through to the bone, about 10 minutes in total for each piece, depending on the size. Transfer to the paper towels. Turn each wing piece over on the paper in order to ensure that excess oil is absorbed from both sides, using additional paper towels as necessary to drain thoroughly.

5. When all of the chicken is cooked and drained, remove the paper towels from the platter, sprinkle the chicken with salt, and serve immediately.

TART CHICKEN ALLA CACCIATORA

Serves 4

Alla cacciatore, meaning "cooked the hunter's way," probably once described methods for cooking game, but Italians use the term today to mean any number of stovetop methods for cooking every kind of meat, domesticated or otherwise. No doubt it was the hunter's wife who did the cooking. Such is the case at Ristorante Cibocchi, a little out-of-the-way *trattoria* in the region of Umbria where the owner's aunt is behind the stove. Her version of chicken *alla cacciatora* is a zesty combination of chopped lemon, peel and all, fresh rosemary, and sage.

3½-POUND FREE-RANGE OR ORGANIC CHICKEN, INCLUDING GIBLETS, CUT UP

6 TABLESPOONS EXTRA-VIRGIN OLIVE OIL

5 CLOVES GARLIC, CUT INTO SMALL PIECES

½ ONION, CHOPPED

2 TEASPOONS MINCED FRESH ROSEMARY, OR 1 TEASPOON CRUMBLED DRIED ROSEMARY

1 TEASPOON MINCED FRESH SAGE, OR ½ TEASPOON CRUMBLED DRIED SAGE

⅓ CUP PITTED, BRINE-CURED TART GREEN OLIVES SUCH AS PICHOLINE, SLICED

½ CUP PLUS 2 TABLESPOONS GOOD-QUALITY DRY WHITE WINE

1½ TABLESPOON WHITE WINE VINEGAR

1 TABLESPOON CAPERS, DRAINED AND MINCED

1 LEMON SLICE, ¼ INCH THICK, SEEDED AND MINCED, INCLUDING PEEL

PINCH OF RED PEPPER FLAKES

½ TEASPOON SEA SALT, OR TO TASTE

1. Rinse the chicken pieces, dry well, and trim off all excess fat. Trim any dark spots, fat, and membrane from the liver and heart and dice. Trim the tough outer layer from the gizzards and chop.

2. In a deep, heavy-bottomed skillet ample enough for all of the chicken pieces without crowding, warm the olive oil over medium-high heat. When it is sizzling hot, add the chicken pieces. Allow them to brown nicely and evenly on all sides, about 15 minutes. Transfer the chicken to a plate and set aside.

3. Drain off a tablespoon or two of the fat from the pan. Add the garlic, onion, rosemary, and sage, all at once. Sauté over low heat until the garlic and onion are thoroughly cooked but not browned, 5 to 7 minutes. Return the chicken to the skillet, and olives. Use a wooden spoon to toss all the ingredients together. Pour in the wine and add the vinegar, capers, lemon, red pepper flakes, and salt. Cover partially and cook until the chicken is done or registers 165°F on an instant-read thermometer, about 20 minutes. Add up to ½ cup water if the chicken dries out.

4. Transfer the chicken and its sauce to a warmed platter and serve immediately.

OVEN-FRIED CHICKEN WITH BREADCRUMBS
Serves 4

I heard about Luisa Petrucci's home cooking from her daughter, who talked so lovingly about her mother's food that I couldn't resist asking for her recipes. Luisa emigrated from Umbria, but learned to cook from her Sicilian mother-in-law. This Sicilian version of oven-fried chicken with its delightfully crunchy coating and moist, tender meat is so similar to deep-fried chicken that you'll hardly be able to tell the difference.

EXTRA-VIRGIN OLIVE OIL

3½-POUND CUT-UP FREE-RANGE OR ORGANIC CHICKEN AND ITS LIVER

1 CUP LIGHTLY TOASTED PANKO CRUMBS OR BREADCRUMBS

¼ CUP FINELY, FRESHLY GRATED PARMIGIANO-REGGIANO, PECORINO ROMANO, OR GRANA PADANO CHEESE

3 LARGE CLOVES GARLIC, MINCED

3 TABLESPOONS MINCED FRESH FLAT-LEAF PARSLEY

1 TEASPOON SEA SALT

FRESHLY GROUND BLACK PEPPER

3 LARGE EGGS, BEATEN

1 TEASPOON MILK

1. Preheat an oven to 350°F. Grease an ample baking pan with olive oil.

2. Trim excess fat from the chicken pieces and discard. Trim any fat or membranes from the liver. Wash the chicken and pat dry with absorbent paper towels. Keep the wing tips intact and cut the wings at the joint to separate the drummettes.

3. Combine the bread crumbs, grated cheese, garlic, parsley, salt, and pepper to taste and spread on a sheet of wax paper or on a platter. Beat the eggs and milk in a wide bowl next to the wax paper. Roll the chicken pieces in the crumb mixture. Dip each piece in the beaten egg and roll once again in the crumb mixture. Arrange them in the baking pan. Drizzle evenly with olive oil.

4. Bake the chicken until golden and cooked through, about 30 minutes for breast pieces and 40 minutes for dark meat, or until an instant-read meat thermometer registers 160°F. Be careful not to overcook. Allow the chicken to settle for 10 minutes before serving hot.

DONATELLA PLATONI'S
ANGRY CHICKEN
Serves 4

My friend Donatella Platoni comes from farming stock, so when she invited me to her country house near Perugia to eat *pollo all'arrabbiata,* a signature local dish, I wasn't surprised to hear her reprimanding her butcher about some chickens he had just delivered. She had placed an order for the slaughtered birds to include the stomachs as proof that they had been fed grain. The stomachs of these birds showed no trace of grain, so she sent them back and a fresh batch with grain-filled stomachs was delivered to the house within the hour.

2 YOUNG FREE-RANGE OR ORGANIC POUSSINS WITH GIBLETS, 1½ TO 2 POUNDS EACH, CUT INTO SERVING PIECES, OR 1 LARGER FREE-RANGE OR ORGANIC CHICKEN WITH GIBLETS, ABOUT 3½ POUNDS, CUT INTO SERVING PIECES

5 TABLESPOONS EXTRA-VIRGIN OLIVE OIL

½ SMALL ONION, CUT INTO WEDGES WITH CORE ATTACHED

6 LARGE CLOVES GARLIC, CRUSHED

1 SMALL DRIED HOT RED PEPPER, OR ¼ TEASPOON OR MORE RED PEPPER FLAKES

1 TEASPOON MINCED FRESH ROSEMARY OR ½ TEASPOON CRUMBLED DRIED ROSEMARY

½ CUP DRY WHITE WINE

1 CUP PEELED, SEEDED, AND CHOPPED PLUM TOMATOES, DRAINED

½ TEASPOON SEA SALT, OR TO TASTE

1. Rinse the chicken pieces and dry well. Trim any dark spots, fat, and membrane from the liver(s) and heart(s) and cut into quarters. Trim the tough outer layer from the gizzard(s), then chop. Set all aside.

2. In a cold, deep, heavy-bottomed nonstick skillet, ample enough to fit the chicken without crowding (or sauté in two batches), warm the olive oil. Add the chicken and giblets, raise the heat to medium, and sauté until browned nicely on all sides, about 20 minutes. Transfer to a platter and set aside.

3. Add the onion, garlic, whole pepper or red pepper flakes, and rosemary and sauté gently until the garlic and onion are softened but not browned, about 8 minutes.

4. Return the chicken to the pan and pour in the wine. Stir all the ingredients together, taking care not to tear the chicken pieces. Use a metal spatula to gently detach any piece that may stick to the bottom of the pan, so as to leave all the pieces intact. When the alcohol has evaporated, after about 3 minutes, distribute the tomatoes evenly in the pan. Reduce the heat to medium-low and cook until the chicken is tender and registers 165°F on an instant-read meat thermometer, about 20 minutes. Season with the salt and transfer to a warmed platter. Serve hot.

TURKEY MEATBALLS
WITH LEMON SAUCE

Serves 4 to 6

Making meatballs with turkey or chicken can be tricky because unlike beef, poultry dries out easily when it is overcooked by even a few seconds. There are two keys to keeping the meat moist during cooking. First, because breast meat toughens easily, it is best to use dark meat. Second, keep the heat low during cooking. In my family, a favorite accompaniment to these meatballs is Creamy Mashed Potatoes with Garlic (page 173).

2 SLICES WHITE BREAD, CRUSTS REMOVED

MILK, FOR SOAKING

2 TABLESPOONS EXTRA-VIRGIN OLIVE OIL

4 SHALLOTS, MINCED

1 POUND GROUND TURKEY DARK MEAT

2 OUNCES PANCETTA, MINCED (OPTIONAL)

1 LARGE EGG, BEATEN

¼ CUP FRESHLY GRATED PARMIGIANO-REGGIANO OR GRANA PADANO CHEESE

¼ TEASPOON FRESHLY GRATED NUTMEG

1 TEASPOON SEA SALT

FRESHLY GROUND BLACK PEPPER

½ CUP ALL-PURPOSE FLOUR

4 TABLESPOONS (½ STICK) UNSALTED BUTTER

½ CUP WINE

1 CUP CHICKEN BROTH (PAGE 214), OR AS NEEDED

FRESHLY SQUEEZED JUICE OF 1 LEMON

1. In a small bowl, cover the bread with milk until soaked; squeeze dry and set aside.

2. Warm 1 tablespoon of the olive oil in a small skillet and sauté the shallots over medium heat until softened, about 3 minutes.

3. In a mixing bowl, combine the turkey, bread, sautéed shallots, pancetta (if using), egg, cheese, nutmeg, salt, and pepper. Form a small meat patty and fry it to check for seasoning. Chill the mixture for at least an hour before forming into 1-inch meatballs. Just before cooking, dredge them lightly in flour and shake off excess.

4. In a skillet, melt the butter with the remaining tablespoon olive oil. Sauté the meatballs over medium-low to medium heat in one layer, browning them gently all over. When an instant-read thermometer inserted into the center registers 160°F, the meatballs are done, about 8 minutes. Transfer to a warm plate.

5. When all the meatballs are cooked, add the wine to the pan, and scrape up any bits of meat. Stir in the chicken broth and simmer until a creamy sauce is formed, about 3 minutes. Strain through a sieve, and add salt and pepper to taste. Whisk in the lemon juice. Add the meatballs to the sauce and heat through gently over low heat, turning occasionally, about 2 minutes. Adjust for salt and pepper and serve.

CHAPTER
7

MAIN DISHES:
MEAT

Economical cuts, stewed or braised in a rich bath fortified with wine or vinegar, are popular in Italian homes, as are veal, pork, and grass-fed beef, cooked with aromatics in olive oil or sometimes butter, and thin, breaded fried cutlets. Roasted and grilled meats grace the family table as well, and lamb in particular is appreciated for its robust flavor and Christian symbolism. (The lamb on the shoulder of Christ the Good Shepherd represents a soul going home to God.) Each spring of my youth my parents went to rural Pennsylvania to buy milk-fed baby lamb for Easter. The trip recalled my mother's childhood in Sardinia, where, as all over Italy, a true baby lamb is not a day over six weeks. Delicate, buttery, and fork-tender, it's much superior to ordinary spring lamb. Some of the recipes in this chapter are actually Italian-American, but there are also original and surprising dishes that are unknown except to the fortunate families of the home cooks who taught them to me.

MOIST PAN-FRIED PORK CHOPS
WITH CRUNCHY CRUMB AND FENNEL COATING

Serves 4

Here are my aunt Rita's delicious pork chops, moist inside with a crispy fennel crust. For best and most wholesome results, buy "natural" pork. Industrially raised pork is injected with liquid, which interferes with proper browning. The secret to the success of these chops is to not overcook them; follow directions precisely for good results. The best accompaniments are Creamy Mashed Potatoes with Garlic (page 173) and Anna Amendolara Nurse's braised cabbage with garlic, pancetta, and hot red pepper (see page 167).

¼ CUP BREAD CRUMBS OR PANKO

2 TABLESPOONS FENNEL SEEDS

½ TEASPOON SEA SALT

FRESHLY GROUND BLACK PEPPER

½ TEASPOON EXTRA-VIRGIN OLIVE OIL FOR BRUSHING ON MEAT, PLUS 3 TABLESPOONS FOR FRYING

4 BONELESS CENTER-CUT PORK CHOPS (1¼ POUNDS), NO MORE THAN ¾ INCH THICK

1. Preheat an oven to 200°F. Spread the bread crumbs or panko on a sheet pan and slide them onto the middle rack of the oven. Bake until faintly colored but not at all brown, about 7 minutes. Warm the fennel seeds in a frying pan over medium-low heat until their aroma is released, about 2 minutes. Transfer to a spice mill and grind to a semi-fine texture; there should still be just the slightest roughness.

2. Combine the toasted bread crumbs with the ground fennel seeds, salt, and pepper to taste, and spread out on a piece of wax paper. Pound the chops lightly on both sides to a thickness of ½ inch. Blot both sides with paper towels. Brush the chops with the ½ teaspoon olive oil. Just before cooking, dredge the chops in the crumb mixture and press into the surface with the palm of your hand.

3. Warm a shallow 12-inch cast-iron skillet or nonstick frying pan over medium heat. When a drop of water skitters on the surface, after about 4 minutes, pour in the 3 tablespoons olive oil. When it is sizzling hot, place the chops in the pan, pressing each with your fingers to provide immediate contact. Cook over medium heat until golden on the first side, about 2 minutes. Use a spatula to flip the chops over and turn off the heat. Cover the pan tightly and allow the chops to rest, covered, until an instant-read meat thermometer inserted into the center registers 130°F, about 3 minutes. Remove the cover and increase the heat to medium. Brown to crisp on both sides, about 2 minutes in total, using a spatula to carefully turn the meat to prevent the crispy coating from sticking to the pan surface. Transfer the chops to a warm platter, tent lightly with foil, and let rest for 5 minutes before serving.

SAUTÉED SWEET PORK SAUSAGES
WITH ROASTED BLACK GRAPES

Serves 4

I learned to pair pork sausages and grapes in Umbria during the harvest when the wine grape is in abundance and quick and hearty dishes are prepared for the workers laboring in the vineyards. In the traditional recipe (see Note, below), the grapes are cooked in a cast-iron skillet along with the sausages, but I've gotten into the habit of roasting the grapes separately, which sears and caramelizes them and concentrates their flavors more. You can do this in a toaster oven rather than heating up a large oven for such a small amount of fruit. Either way you cook them, it's a lovely dish. You might serve it with Basic Polenta (page 217) and Anna Maria's Roasted Onions with Crumb Topping (page 172), followed by Warm Winter Greens Salad with Bacon Vinaigrette (page 64).

8 SWEET ITALIAN PORK SAUSAGES

½ CUP WATER

¾ POUND SEEDLESS BLACK OR RED GRAPES, STRIPPED FROM THEIR STEMS

COOKING OIL SPRAY OR OLIVE OIL

1. Use a sharp knife or fork to poke a few holes in the sausages before cooking them. Select a seasoned cast-iron skillet or other heavy-bottomed pan. Put the sausages and the water in the skillet and place on a burner over medium heat. When the water has evaporated and the sausages have begun to color lightly, after about 12 minutes, reduce the heat to medium-low and continue to cook the sausages, pricking them occasionally to release excess fat, until they are browned all over and cooked through, about 20 minutes more. (Do not prick them too much, or they will dry out.)

2. For the grapes, preheat a toaster oven or an oven to 375°F. Wash and dry the grapes well. Oil them very lightly with cooking oil spray or toss them in a bowl with a touch of olive oil. Spread them out on the toaster oven pan or on a baking sheet and roast until brown and bubbly, about 15 minutes. Note that they can burn easily because of their high sugar content, so keep an eye on them as they cook.

3. Transfer the sausages and grapes to a large warmed platter, leaving behind any fat, and serve immediately.

NOTE: If you would like to cook the grapes in the pan alongside the sausages, add them to the skillet when the sausage cooking water has evaporated and the sausages have begun to color lightly, after about 12 minutes. Proceed as directed for the remainder of the method.

ZIA RITA'S
STUFFED BEEF BRACIOLE

Serves 4

My aunt Rita Ghisu came from Cagliari. Her cooking is like her, elegant and refined—like these braciole stuffed with mortadella, pistachios, savory crumbs, and grated Parmigiano-Reggiano cheese. Use flank steak or thin slices of rump steak pounded ¼ inch thick.

2½-POUND FLANK STEAK, ¾ INCH THICK, PARTIALLY FROZEN

¼ CUP CHOPPED, TOASTED SHELLED PISTACHIOS

6 LARGE CLOVES GARLIC, CHOPPED

2 MEDIUM SHALLOTS, MINCED

5 TABLESPOONS CHOPPED FRESH FLAT-LEAF PARSLEY

6 TABLESPOONS FRESHLY GRATED PARMIGIANO-REGGIANO OR GRANA PADANO CHEESE

12 THIN SLICES IMPORTED MORTADELLA, OR PROSCIUTTO

4 TABLESPOONS EXTRA-VIRGIN OLIVE OIL

1 TABLESPOON UNSALTED BUTTER

2 28-OUNCE CANS CRUSHED ITALIAN PLUM TOMATOES

2 TEASPOONS SEA SALT

1 CUP GOOD-QUALITY DRY RED WINE

FRESHLY GROUND BLACK PEPPER

COTTON BUTCHER'S TWINE OR STRONG TOOTHPICKS

1. Butterfly the steak and pound it to a ¼-inch-thickness. Place the steak cut side up with the grain parallel to the edge of your counter edge. Cut into 12 pieces, each 3 x 4 inches. Distribute the pistachios, garlic, shallots, parsley, and grated cheese over each. Then roll a slice of mortadella into a cigar shape and place it in the center of each piece of meat so that it lies in the same direction as the grain. Roll up each bundle of meat tightly and tie it securely with butcher's twine. Alternatively, use toothpicks to keep the rolls closed. The rolls should be neither overly tight nor overly loose.

2. In a Dutch oven that is large enough to accommodate all the braciole at once without crowding, warm the olive oil and butter together. When it is hot enough to sear the meat, slip the braciole into the pan. If the pan is not large enough, sear in two batches. Brown the braciole on all sides over medium-high heat, about 15 minutes. Lower the heat to medium-low and add the tomatoes and salt to the pan. Partially cover and simmer over the lowest heat so that barely a bubble breaks the surface, about 1 hour. Add the wine and continue to simmer until the meat is very tender, about 2½ hours.

3. Add pepper to taste and check for seasoning. Allow the braciole to settle for 15 minutes before serving. Remove the string or toothpicks. Serve the sauce over freshly cooked polenta, rice, macaroni, or strand-type pasta. Serve the braciole separately as a second course.

NONNA VERA'S
TENDER AND CRUNCHY BEEF MEDALLIONS

Serves 4

I learned this wonderful recipe from my Italian friend Anna Maria Erenbourg Weld. It is a recipe from her grandmother, Vera Ehrenbourg D'Angara. Nonna Vera always served them with sweet and sour carrots (page 164). Keep in mind that because the medallions (patties) have a crunchy surface but remain tender and juicy within, they should be neither undercooked nor overcooked. For best results, follow the directions carefully.

MILK	1 EXTRA-LARGE EGG
2 SLICES STALE ARTISAN BREAD, CRUSTS REMOVED, SHREDDED, YIELDING 1 CUP	1 TEASPOON SEA SALT, PLUS MORE FOR SPRINKLING
1 CUP BREAD CRUMBS FOR COATING MEAT PATTIES, PLUS ⅛ CUP	¼ TEASPOON FRESHLY GROUND BLACK PEPPER
3 TABLESPOONS EXTRA-VIRGIN OLIVE OIL	1 POUND GROUND, LEAN ORGANIC OR NATURE-RAISED BEEF
1 SMALL ONION, MINCED	
¼ CUP ALL-PURPOSE FLOUR	PURE OLIVE OIL, FOR FRYING

1. In a small bowl, pour enough milk to cover the shredded bread. When completely soaked, squeeze the milk out but keep the bread moist. Discard the milk. Spread the cup of bread crumbs on a large piece of wax paper.

2. In a large skillet, warm the extra-virgin olive oil. Add the onion and sauté until softened, about 4 minutes. Sprinkle on the flour and stir. When the flour has absorbed the oil and coated the onions, after about 3 minutes, let the mixture cool.

3. In a mixing bowl, beat the egg with the salt and pepper. Add the ground beef, the ⅛ cup bread crumbs, onions, and bread, crumbled. Wet your hands and blend the mixture very thoroughly. Form patties about 2 inches in diameter and ¼ inch thick resembling large, round coins. Pat the sides to create a straight coin-like edge rather than a sloped edge. Use a knife to score each medallion with a tic-tac-toe on both sides, (this will allow the patties to form a lovely crunchy surface while the center remains moist). Just before frying, dredge in bread crumbs, shaking off excess.

4. Wipe out your skillet. Pour in enough olive oil to reach halfway up the sides of the patties. Warm the oil over medium heat. When it is sizzling hot, slip the patties in, allowing plenty of room around each for proper searing. Cook over medium heat until nicely browned and crunchy on the surface, about 15 minutes. Resist the temptation to press down on the patties as they cook; doing this will make the patties dry and hard. Drain on paper towels and sprinkle lightly with salt while hot.

CLASSIC MEATBALLS

Serves 8

These savory little delicacies are typically browned in oil, then transferred to a pot of tomato sauce to finish cooking. But they can also be served "nude," meaning without sauce. In summer, I like to impale them on sturdy twigs of fresh rosemary after they are cooked and serve them as appetizers.

1 CUP CUBED STALE WHITE BREAD, CRUSTS REMOVED (ABOUT 2 SLICES)

½ CUP MILK OR TASTY MEAT BROTH (PAGE 213)

1 POUND LEAN GROUND BEEF

½ POUND LEAN GROUND PORK

2 OUNCES PROSCIUTTO, MINCED

1 SMALL ONION, GRATED ON THE LARGE OVAL HOLES OF A BOX GRATER

1 FRESH PLUM TOMATO, PEELED, SEEDED, AND MINCED

3 CLOVES GARLIC, GRATED

2 TEASPOONS CHOPPED FRESH MARJORAM, OR 1 TEASPOON CRUMBLED DRIED MARJORAM

1 EXTRA-LARGE EGG, LIGHTLY BEATEN

2 TEASPOONS SEA SALT, PLUS MORE TO TASTE

FRESHLY GROUND BLACK PEPPER

PURE OLIVE OIL, FOR FRYING

ALL-PURPOSE FLOUR, FOR DREDGING

1. Put the bread in a small bowl and add the milk or broth. When the bread is softened thoroughly, squeeze dry, discarding the liquid, and place it in a bowl. Add the ground meats, prosciutto, onion, tomato, garlic, marjoram, egg, 2 teaspoons salt, and pepper to taste. Using your hands, blend the mixture well. Make a small patty and fry it to check for seasoning. Form into walnut-size meatballs.

2. Pour the oil to a depth of ½ inch into a large, wide skillet and place over medium heat. Spread the flour onto an ample sheet of wax paper. Lightly dredge as many meatballs as you will fry in the first batch. When the oil is hot enough to make the meatballs sizzle upon contact, slip them into the pan one at a time, being careful not to crowd the pan. Fry over medium heat until nicely browned all over and cooked through, about 10 minutes.

3. Using tongs or a slotted spatula, transfer to paper towels to drain, then place on a platter and keep warm. Taste for salt and, if necessary, sprinkle salt sparingly over the meatballs. Serve hot or warm.

TOMATO SAUCE VARIATION: To prepare the meatballs in tomato sauce, prepare a double recipe of any of the meatless tomato sauces in chapter 2. Cook the meatballs as directed, then simmer together with the sauce over low heat for 20 minutes before serving.

JUICY MEAT LOAF
WITH TOMATO AND RED WINE GLAZE

Serves 8

Italian meat loaf is delicately seasoned and almost always made with several kinds of meat. I've gotten into the habit of working a little minced fresh tomato into the mixture, which helps to keep it moist. Toward the end of cooking, the pan juices are fortified with tomato puree and wine to form a delicious sauce. Serve this succulent meat loaf for dinner, or leftover at room temperature; it is equally good hot or cold.

6 SLICES STALE WHITE BREAD WITH CRUSTS REMOVED, SHREDDED

MILK OR TASTY MEAT BROTH (PAGE 213)

2 TABLESPOONS OLIVE OIL

2 ONIONS, MINCED

2 LARGE CLOVES GARLIC, MINCED

3 TABLESPOONS BREAD CRUMBS

3 LARGE EGGS, BEATEN

2 TEASPOONS SEA SALT

1½ TEASPOONS FRESHLY GROUND BLACK PEPPER

½ CUP FRESHLY GRATED PARMIGIANO-REGGIANO OR GRANA PADANO CHEESE

6 TABLESPOONS MINCED FRESH FLAT-LEAF PARSLEY

1 TABLESPOON MINCED FRESH THYME, OR 2 TEASPOONS CRUSHED DRIED THYME

3 POUNDS MIXED LEAN GROUND BEEF AND PORK, OR 3 POUNDS LEAN GROUND BEEF

4 OUNCES SOPRESSATA, MINCED

2 LARGE, FIRM, FRESH TOMATOES, PEELED, SEEDED, AND MINCED

6 TABLESPOONS TASTY MEAT BROTH (PAGE 213) OR WATER

½ CUP GOOD-QUALITY DRY RED WINE

3 CUPS TOMATO SAUCE

1. Preheat an oven to 350°F. Soak the bread in enough milk or broth to cover. Squeeze it dry and discard the liquid. Shred the dampened bread well and set aside.

2. In a skillet, warm the olive oil and sauté the onion and garlic over medium heat until soft, about 7 minutes; cool.

3. In the meantime, scatter the bread crumbs on an approximate 12 x 18-inch work surface. Grease a 9 x 13-inch baking dish.

4. In an ample mixing bowl, lightly beat the eggs with the salt, pepper, grated cheese, parsley, and thyme. Add the meat(s), soppressata, shredded bread, sautéed onion mixture, and minced tomato. Wet your hands and thoroughly blend all the ingredients together. Spread the meat mixture on the bread crumb–covered work surface, using your hands to form a typical long and narrow log-shaped loaf. Place the meat loaf in the baking dish and sprinkle 3 tablespoons of the broth or water around it.

5. Slide the meatloaf onto the middle rack of the oven and bake for 50 minutes, or until an instant-read meat thermometer registers at 160°F, adding the remaining stock or water after 15 minutes. Baste several times during baking with the pan juices, adding a little more water if the juices seem to be drying up; no more than a tablespoon or two, if any, should be necessary. There should be sufficient juice in the baking pan to keep the meat loaf moist and to guarantee pan juices when it is done. Fifteen minutes before the meat is cooked, add the wine to the pan and pour the tomato sauce over the top to glaze the surface. When done, remove the meat loaf from the oven, tent with foil, and let rest for 15 minutes. Pass the sauce and drippings that have formed in the pan through a sieve into a saucepan, and heat through over low heat, stirring to blend. Taste and adjust for seasoning.

6. Cut the meat loaf into ¾-inch-thick slices. Overlap them on a serving platter or individual plates. Moisten with the sauce and serve, passing more sauce at the table.

LONG-SIMMERED BEEF STEW
WITH CLOVES AND RED WINE

Serves 4

Called *stracotto* in Italian, this richly flavored stew is often the mainstay of Sunday supper. It produces plenty of pan juices, which also makes it ideal to serve with bread, steaming polenta (see page 217), or pureed potatoes. The cooking method is much in the style of the famous beef stew of Burgundy, resulting in butter-tender meat and an intoxicatingly rich, winey sauce—excellent cold-weather food.

3 POUNDS STEWING BEEF, TRIMMED OF EXCESS FAT AND CUBED

5 TABLESPOONS EXTRA-VIRGIN OLIVE OIL

4 OUNCES PORK FATBACK, CUT INTO MATCHSTICK STRIPS

2 ONIONS, CHOPPED

5 LARGE CLOVES GARLIC, SMASHED

2 BAY LEAVES

1 TEASPOON MINCED FRESH MARJORAM, OR ½ TEASPOON CRUMBLED DRIED MARJORAM

½ TEASPOON GROUND CLOVES

3 CARROTS, CUT INTO DICE

3-INCH STRIP OF LEMON ZEST

1½ TEASPOONS SEA SALT, OR TO TASTE

FRESHLY GROUND BLACK PEPPER

3 TABLESPOONS ALL-PURPOSE FLOUR

3 TABLESPOONS TOMATO PASTE

¾ CUP GOOD-QUALITY, FULL-BODIED DRY RED WINE, SUCH AS CHIANTI

1. Preheat an oven to 450°F. Blot the meat well with paper towels.

2. In an ample Dutch oven with a wide pan surface, warm 3 tablespoons of the olive oil over medium heat and add the fatback; sauté until lightly browned, 2 to 3 minutes. Use a slotted spoon to transfer it to a dish and set aside. Add the beef in two batches to the pan and brown it on all sides, about 12 minutes. Transfer the beef to the dish with the fatback. Wipe the pan with a paper towel.

3. Add 2 more tablespoons olive oil to the pan and stir in the onion, garlic, bay leaves, marjoram, cloves, carrots, and lemon zest. Sauté until lightly colored and aromatic, about 6 minutes. Return the beef and the fatback to the pan, season with salt and pepper, and stir. Sprinkle the flour over the meat. Stir in the tomato paste mixed with a little water, then the wine and enough water to barely cover the meat. Cover and cook over low heat until the meat is tender, about 2 hours. Add water as needed to prevent the meat from drying out and to ensure plenty of pan juices. Keep the liquid at half the height of the meat. Stir occasionally.

4. When the meat is done, remove the bay leaves and lemon zest. Taste for seasoning and serve.

VEAL STEW
WITH LEMON, ROSEMARY, AND PINE NUT SAUCE

Serves 4

This is one of my mother's stew recipes, invented one night when there were veal steaks left over from a meat stock. This was designed for an economy cut of veal that will stand up to lengthy cooking; a shoulder cut is ideal. Adding pine nuts provides interesting texture and a nutty flavor. Slow braising produces enough gravy for a half pound of fresh egg noodles, Saffron Fregula (page 88), or a heap of Creamy Mashed Potatoes with Garlic (page 173).

5 1-INCH-THICK BONELESS VEAL SHOULDER STEAKS (12 OUNCES EACH)

5 TABLESPOONS ALL-PURPOSE FLOUR

3 TABLESPOONS UNSALTED BUTTER

2 TABLESPOONS EXTRA-VIRGIN OLIVE OIL

⅔ CUP GOOD-QUALITY DRY WHITE WINE

1 TABLESPOON FRESH ROSEMARY, OR 1 TEASPOON CRUSHED DRIED ROSEMARY

2 CUPS CHICKEN BROTH (PAGE 214)

3 2-INCH STRIPS LEMON PEEL, ZEST ONLY

½ TEASPOON SALT, OR TO TASTE

2 TABLESPOONS COARSELY CHOPPED, LIGHTLY TOASTED PINE NUTS

½ TEASPOON FRESHLY GROUND WHITE OR BLACK PEPPER

1. Trim excess fat from the veal and cut each steak in half. If there is bone, include it in the dish, as it will add flavor to the sauce and can be sucked for the marrow like a miniature osso bucco. Spread the flour on a piece of wax paper.

2. Heat half of the butter and olive oil together in a deep skillet until sizzling hot. Dredge half of the veal in the flour and slip into the skillet. Brown over moderately high heat, turning once, until nicely colored on both sides, about 15 minutes. Transfer to a platter and repeat with the remaining butter, oil, and veal, as above.

3. Add the wine and rosemary to the skillet and cook, stirring with a wooden spoon, until the wine evaporates, about 1 minute. Stir in about ⅓ cup of the broth. Return the veal to the skillet in a single layer, cover, and simmer over moderately low heat until the broth is absorbed, about 10 minutes. Stir in ¼-cup measurements of broth at 10-minute intervals, or as needed, to keep the meat moist.

4. After 1 hour, add the lemon zest. Continue to cook the veal over low heat, covered, until tender, another 45 to 60 minutes. Continue to add the remaining stock at 10-minute intervals as necessary. Stir in the salt and pine nuts 15 minutes before the meat is done. Stir in the pepper and serve.

AHEAD-OF-TIME NOTE: The stew can be refrigerated for up to 3 days. Rewarm over low heat, stirring in about ¼ cup extra chicken broth.

ROMAN BRAISED LAMB
WITH WHITE WINE AND ARTICHOKES

Serves 4

Here is a dish adapted from a recipe given to me by my Swedish-born friend, Clarisse Schiller, who has lived in Italy for most of her life. She learned how to cook the lusty dishes of the Roman countryside from her mother-in-law, and passed many of them on to me. I especially like this one because I am fond of the combination of lamb and artichokes. The artichokes should be fresh and once they are cleaned, the rest of the preparation is quite simple. The thick, aromatic gravy calls for serving the stew with plenty of sturdy bread, polenta, or crostini. Offer good dry red wine at the table, too.

ZEST OF 1 LEMON AND JUICE OF 2 LEMONS

6 FRESH MEDIUM ARTICHOKES, OR 10 FRESH BABY ARTICHOKES

2 POUNDS (TRIMMED WEIGHT) LAMB SHOULDER OR OTHER STEWING CUT OF LAMB, INCLUDING SOME BONE

½ CUP ALL-PURPOSE FLOUR

3 TABLESPOONS EXTRA-VIRGIN OLIVE OIL

3 LARGE CLOVES GARLIC, CRUSHED

1 CARROT, SHREDDED ON THE LARGE

HOLES OF A BOX GRATER

¾ TEASPOON SEA SALT, OR TO TASTE

½ CUP DRY WHITE WINE

1½ CUPS CHICKEN BROTH, PLUS MORE IF NEEDED (PAGE 214)

THREE 6-INCH SPRIGS FRESH DILL, OR 3 TABLESPOONS MINCED FRESH FENNEL FRONDS

FRESHLY GROUND BLACK PEPPER

1. Add about 6 inches of water to a large glass or ceramic bowl, then squeeze the juice of one of the lemons into it. Trim a thin slice from the bottom of the stem of each artichoke. Pare off all the dark green skin on the stem. With one hand, pull off the tough outer leaves until you reach leaves with tender white areas at their base. Using a serrated knife, cut off the upper dark green part of the inner leaves; leave the light base. (If you decide to use baby artichokes, there will be fewer tough outer leaves to remove.) Cut the artichoke in half lengthwise and, with a small knife, cut out the hairy choke and any other tough inner purple leaves. As each artichoke is finished, immediately put it in the lemon water to prevent it from turning brown. (Once cleaned, the artichokes can remain in the lemon water in the refrigerator for up to 24 hours.) When all of the artichokes have been trimmed, drain them, cut each half in half again, and pat dry. Place each artichoke half, cut side down, on a cutting board, and cut into quarters lengthwise. Cook the sliced artichoke hearts in boiling water to cover for 10 minutes. Drain and set aside.

2. Trim the excess fat from the lamb, but leave the bones, which will add to the flavor of the stew. Cut the meat into approximate 1½-inch pieces. Place the lamb in a

bowl with 2 inches of cold water to cover and the remaining lemon juice. Use your hands to squeeze out excess blood, then leave it to soak for 30 minutes. Drain the meat, rinse, and pat thoroughly dry with clean kitchen towels.

3. Scatter the lemon zest on a piece of wax paper the size of a cutting board, and roll the meat in it. Spread the meat out on your work surface in a single layer. Sprinkle it lightly with the flour and shake off any excess.

4. In a large, heavy skillet or Dutch oven, warm the olive oil over medium heat and add the lamb. Brown nicely all over, about 12 minutes. Add the garlic, carrot, and salt. Stir in the wine. Cook to evaporate, about 2 minutes. Cover halfway with the broth, reduce the heat to low, partially cover, and cook, adding more broth a little at a time as needed, until the lamb is tender, about 1¼ hours, depending on the cut of the meat. Check the pot frequently to prevent the meat from drying out. When the meat is almost done, add the artichoke hearts and cover. Cook over low heat until the artichoke hearts are tender and the flavors of all the ingredients marry, another 10 to 15 minutes. Stir in the dill or fennel and season with pepper.

8

MAIN DISHES:
SEAFOOD

"Mangiamo il pesce!"—"Let's have fish!"—my cousins cried whenever I visited them in Cagliari. Whether cooked at home or eaten at a restaurant near the beach, a seafood meal was a treat. This wasn't always the case in Sardinia, which is a lush garden in the middle of the sea. If you were to have visited there before Mussolini's time, before the malaria-infested swamps along the coastline were drained, you wouldn't have gone anywhere near the sea. But the island's seafood was astonishingly good, prepared simply with the fragrant local olive oil and perhaps saffron, wild marjoram, and wild fennel. Many such memories are tucked away in the happy reaches of my mind. I know only too well how special these seafood dinners were, and now how rare. Today, even in Italy, most fish is farmed because some species are overfished and others tainted by high levels of mercury. Nevertheless, many excellent dishes can be made with what is available. The Italian way with seafood is to keep it simple, such as the dishes included here.

OVEN-FRIED TILAPIA
WITH FENNEL CRUST

Serves 4

The Mediterranean combination of fish and fennel is a marriage made in heaven, especially in this crunchy-crusted tilapia creation I originally invented for schoolchildren. Once introduced to their repertoire, it became one of the all-time favorites on the lunch menu—for children and adults alike, even among the less sophisticated eaters who thought they didn't like fish.

1¼ CUPS BREAD CRUMBS OR PANKO

1 TEASPOON FRESHLY, FINELY GROUND FENNEL SEEDS

½ TEASPOON CRUSHED DRIED THYME

1 CUP EXTRA-VIRGIN OLIVE OIL

4 FRESH TILAPIA FILLETS (ABOUT 2 POUNDS), EACH CUT DOWN THE MIDDLE AND SLICED INTO A TOTAL OF 6 PIECES

4 TABLESPOONS DIJON MUSTARD

1. Preheat an oven to 200°F. Spread the bread crumbs out on a sheet pan and slide them onto the middle rack of the oven. Bake until faintly colored but not at all brown, about 7 minutes. Remove and cool.

2. Increase the oven temperature to 350°F. Spray a baking sheet with cooking spray.

3. In a shallow bowl, combine the bread crumbs with the herbs and the olive oil. Using a pastry brush, paint the fish pieces with a thin film of the mustard. Then coat each piece with the bread crumb mixture and transfer to the baking sheet, leaving plenty of room between each piece for heat to circulate around it.

4. Bake until cooked through but still moist and tender, about 10 minutes. (Note: Cooking time is accurate for small, cut-up fillet pieces. For larger pieces, cook longer.) Arrange 6 pieces of the fillets on each individual plate and serve at once.

FISH FILLETS WITH CRISPY SAGE LEAVES

Serves 4

This elegantly simple recipe was discovered by my friend's brother, Luciano Erenbourg, during a summer in his Otranto home on the Adriatic. There, the gilt-head bream is used for sautéing in this manner, but outside of Italy, we can substitute other firm-fleshed fish. Tilapia is very accessible, inexpensive, and free of mercury and parasites, so it is my fish fillet of choice for this method.

4 FRESH TILAPIA FILLETS (ABOUT 2 POUNDS TOTAL)

SEA SALT AND FRESHLY GROUND BLACK OR WHITE PEPPER

3 TABLESPOONS EXTRA-VIRGIN OLIVE OIL

20 MEDIUM-SIZE FRESH SAGE LEAVES

1. Season the fish with salt and pepper on both sides.

2. Warm a wide, shallow cast-iron skillet over medium-high heat. When a drop of water skitters on the surface, after about 3 minutes, add the olive oil. Tilt the pan to coat the bottom evenly and place the sage leaves on the bottom of the pan. Heat until the oil is almost smoking, about 30 seconds.

3. Lay the fish fillets on top of the sage leaves. If the pan is not large enough to accommodate all the fillets, cook them in two batches. Sear until lightly browned on the bottom, about 3 minutes. Flip each piece over. Reduce the heat to medium and sear until done but still moist, about 2 minutes. Transfer the cooked fillets to a warm plate and repeat the whole process for the second batch, placing fresh sage leaves under each as before. Serve at once.

FRESH TUNA with ONION COMPOTE

Serves 4

When I met Giusepppe Rosso while on a tour of Sicily's olive oil estates, he lamented the erosion of traditional cooking in his region, where his ancestors have produced oil from Tonda Iblea olive groves dating back to the 14th century. This is one of the local dishes his cook made using his prized Villa Zottopera organic oil. The caramelized sweet onions, bathed in tomato and fortified with wine, serve as a bed for the seared tuna steaks. The same treatment given to tuna can be applied to other firm-fleshed fish steaks, including swordfish, cod, and halibut.

4 TUNA FILLETS OR STEAKS
(ABOUT 1½ POUNDS TOTAL)

SEA SALT AND FRESHLY GROUND
BLACK PEPPER

4 TABLESPOONS EXTRA-VIRGIN OLIVE OIL,
PREFERABLY SICILIAN

½ CUP DRY WHITE WINE (PREFERABLY
SICILIAN)

2 LARGE WHITE (SWEET) ONIONS,
QUARTERED AND SLICED THIN

1½ TEASPOONS MINCED FRESH OREGANO,
OR 1 TEASPOON DRIED OREGANO

1½ CUPS CHOPPED FRESH RIPE
TOMATOES

1. Use paper towels to dry the tuna fillets or steaks well and season with salt.

2. Select a seasoned cast-iron skillet or other nonstick skillet that is large enough to accommodate all the fish at once. If you don't have a large enough skillet, sear the fish in smaller batches. Over medium-high heat, pour half of the olive oil in the pan and when it is hot, add the tuna. Sauté the steaks quickly over medium-high heat to sear the surface, about 2 minutes on each side, or until browned lightly on both sides and rare in the middle. Transfer to a platter. Add the wine to the pan and deglaze over medium heat. Pour over the tuna steaks and set aside, keeping the tuna warm.

3. Warm the remaining oil in the same skillet over medium heat. Add the onions and oregano to the pan and sauté over medium-low heat until they are thoroughly softened and nicely colored, about 12 minutes, stirring occasionally for even cooking. Add the chopped tomatoes and simmer over medium heat, stirring occasionally, until the excess liquid evaporates, about 10 minutes. Taste for salt.

4. Return the tuna and its juices to the pan and heat through to finish cooking to taste, being careful not to overcook it. The tuna should be cooked medium to medium-rare and should remain moist and tender inside. Serve at once.

PAN-FRIED TROUT
WITH WHITE WINE AND CAPER SAUCE

Serves 4

When I buy fresh trout in the market, I often cook it this way, a method I learned from a Roman friend. Freshwater fish often needs a flavor boost, accomplished here simply with capers and wine. Newcomers to my table, even the young and the fish-wary, are always delighted with this dish. Have the fishmonger gut and clean the fish and remove the heads so that you will have four fillets with the skin remaining on one side. If increasing the recipe yield, sauté the fillets in batches to avoid overcrowding them in the skillet.

4 BONELESS TROUT FILLET HALVES, SKIN ON (ABOUT 1½ POUNDS TOTAL)

1 CUP ALL-PURPOSE FLOUR

SEA SALT AND FRESHLY GROUND WHITE OR BLACK PEPPER

4 TABLESPOONS (1½ STICKS) UNSALTED BUTTER

4 TABLESPOONS EXTRA-VIRGIN OLIVE OIL

4 TABLESPOONS SMALL CAPERS, DRAINED

½ CUP DRY WHITE WINE

1. Pat the fish dry with paper towels. This step is very important in order to sauté them properly.

2. Place a large piece of wax paper on your work surface and measure the flour onto it. Sprinkle with salt and pepper, then spread the flour out.

3. In a large skillet, melt the butter with the oil over medium heat until it is hot enough to make the fish sizzle. Meanwhile, lightly dredge the trout in the flour. Dredging must be done at the last minute to assure a crisp coating.

4. Slip the trout, skin side down, into the skillet. Do this in batches to ensure plenty of room around each fish for proper sautéing. Pan-fry until the coating is brown, about 3 minutes. Turn the trout over and pan-fry until opaque in the center, about 2 minutes. Transfer the trout to a warm platter.

5. Reduce the heat to medium-low and add the capers and wine to the skillet. Stir to scrape up any browned bits from the bottom of the pan. Cook until the alcohol has evaporated, about 2 minutes. Season with salt. Pour the sauce over the trout fillets and serve at once.

GRILLED WHOLE FISH
IN THE MANNER OF MURANO

Serves 4

The residents of the tiny island of Murano in the Venice lagoon believe that the best way to cook fish is to simply grill or fry it in order not to hamper its pleasureable natural flavor. Here, lemon in company with seafood is considered the height of bad taste since, historically, it was used to disguise stinking fish. Vinegar or white wine and a fresh herb or two is usually all that a Venetian will tolerate. Slices of grilled polenta (see page 217), drizzled with extra-virgin olive oil, make a good accompaniment.

4 PORGIES, STRIPED BASS, OR STRIPED MULLETS, ABOUT 1½ POUNDS EACH, GUTTED AND SCALED

SEA SALT

8 BAY LEAVES

EXTRA-VIRGIN OLIVE OIL

½ CUP WHITE WINE VINEGAR

FRESHLY GROUND PEPPER, PREFERABLY WHITE

1. Preheat a broiler. Alternatively, if cooking on an outdoor grill, prepare a fire and let the wood or coals burn to a white heat. If using a broiler, you will want to place the fish on a preheated rack over a roasting pan so that the heat can circulate on all sides of the fish as it cooks; if cooking over an open fire, you will want to place the fish between two racks, or in a fish "cage," so that they may be turned over easily and without breaking midway through cooking.

2. Rinse the fish and dry well with paper towels. Lightly sprinkle the cavity of each fish with salt, then stuff 2 bay leaves into each. Massage olive oil liberally on both sides of the fish, then sprinkle on half of the vinegar.

3. If broiling, place the fish on the preheated broiling pan about 5 inches under the heat source. Leave the oven door ajar and cook until the fish are golden and crisp on the outside, about 10 minutes. Remove the pan from the broiler, turn the fish over, sprinkle with the remaining vinegar, and slide the pan under the broiler again. Cook for an additional 8 minutes. If cooking over a wood fire, flip over the fish in the racks or cage when the skin is crisp, and cook on the reverse side until done, a total of about 15 minutes. When done, the fish should be opaque throughout when tested with the tip of a knife, and golden on the surface.

4. Discard the bay leaves and season the fish with salt and pepper. Serve at once.

GARLICKY
PAN-ROASTED SHRIMP

Serves 4

Here is one of the easiest and most popular ways for cooking shrimp in Italy and throughout the Mediterranean. In American-Italian cuisine, this recipe would be referred to as "shrimp scampi," a curious title since *scampi* means shrimp and the literal translation, means "shrimp shrimp." Good Italian bread should always be served with this dish for soaking up the delicious sauce.

1 POUND LARGE SHRIMP, PEELED

½ CUP EXTRA-VIRGIN OLIVE OIL

4 LARGE CLOVES GARLIC, CUT INTO SMALL PIECES

PINCH RED PEPPER FLAKES, OR 1 OR 2 WHOLE DRIED PEPERONCINI (HOT PEPPERS)

¼ CUP GOOD-QUALITY DRY WHITE WINE

2 TABLESPOONS CHOPPED FRESH FLAT-LEAF PARSLEY

1 LOAF CRUSTY ARTISAN BREAD, SLICED

1. Remove the dark intestinal veins from the shrimp. As you do, make each cut deep enough to butterfly the shrimp so they can be opened flat, like a book. Rinse under cold running water, drain, and dry thoroughly with a cotton kitchen towel.

2. In a large skillet, warm the oil over medium heat. Add the garlic and red pepper flakes or whole pepper and sauté gently until the garlic has softened but not browned, about 2 minutes. Add the shrimp, placing them opened flat on the bottom of the pan so they do not curl too much; sauté, turning once, until they are opaque, about 2 minutes on each side. Add the wine, stir, and cook for an additional 30 seconds to allow the alcohol to evaporate. Remove the whole pepper, if using. Sprinkle with the parsley and serve immediately. Pass the bread at the table.

BAKED SCAMPI
WITH CRUNCHY CRUMB TOPPING

Serves 4

This is probably one of my favorite shrimp dishes of all for its rosemary-garlic flavor and pleasant, crunchy topping (the Italians call a baked dish with a crunchy bread topping *gratinate*). It is often one of the seven seafood courses I make for *la vigilia,* the traditional feast of seven fishes on Christmas Eve, because it so easy to make and so festive.

2 POUNDS LARGE SHRIMP (OR PRAWNS), PEELED AND DEVEINED

8 TABLESPOONS EXTRA-VIRGIN OLIVE OIL, PLUS MORE FOR GREASING

8 LARGE CLOVES GARLIC, FINELY GRATED

1 TEASPOON MINCED FRESH ROSEMARY LEAVES

2 TEASPOONS MINCED FRESH MARJORAM OR OREGANO

½ TEASPOON RED PEPPER FLAKES

SEA SALT

1½ CUPS PANKO OR PLAIN WHITE BREAD CRUMBS

3 TABLESPOONS CHOPPED FRESH FLAT-LEAF PARSLEY

1 TABLESPOON CHOPPED FRESH CHIVES

½ CUP DRY WHITE WINE

1. Preheat an oven to 400°F. Using a paring knife, make a cut down the back side of each shrimp so that it can lie flat like a book with the tail end standing straight up like a handle.

2. In a bowl, combine half the olive oil, the garlic, rosemary, marjoram or oregano, red pepper flakes, and salt to taste. Add the shrimp and use your hands to work in the seasonings. Cover and chill for 1 to 3 hours.

3. In a separate bowl, mix the panko or bread crumbs, parsley, chives, the remaining 4 tablespoons olive oil, and salt to taste.

4. Select a baking dish large enough to accommodate the shrimp without crowding. Grease lightly with olive oil. Pour in the wine and arrange the shrimp inside, tail facing upward. Sprinkle the bread crumb mixture over the shrimp. Slide the baking pan on the middle rack of the oven and cook until golden, about 15 minutes. Serve at once.

"ANGRY" LOBSTER
BRAISED IN TOMATO SAUCE

Serves 4

This fiery Roman dish has come to be known as "Lobster fra Diavolo," loosely translated as lobster "in company with the devil." The recipe is elementary, but perhaps it will serve as an encouragement to those who never deviate from eating their lobster boiled with drawn butter. Be sure to have good bread at the table for soaking up the splendid sauce.

4 LIVE LOBSTERS (1¼ POUNDS EACH)

6 TABLESPOONS EXTRA-VIRGIN OLIVE OIL

8 LARGE CLOVES GARLIC, CRUSHED

½ TEASPOON RED PEPPER FLAKES

4 TABLESPOONS CHOPPED FRESH FLAT-LEAF PARSLEY

½ TEASPOON CRUSHED DRIED OREGANO

3 CUPS DRAINED CANNED ITALIAN PLUM TOMATOES, SEEDED AND CHOPPED, OR 1 POUND VINE-RIPENED PLUM TOMATOES, PEELED, SEEDED, AND CHOPPED

SCANT ½ TEASPOON SALT, OR TO TASTE

1. Rinse the lobsters in cold water. Kill them humanely in the following way: Place a sharp chef's knife at the point where the body and the head meet on the top of the carapace and quickly drive in the point to sever the spinal cord. Remove the rubber bands that bind the claws. Using the chef's knife, split the lobsters in half lengthwise and pull out the black vein that runs the length of the body. Split each piece in half again crosswise and crack the claws.

2. In very large skillet, warm the olive oil with the garlic over low heat until the garlic is golden but not browned, about 2 minutes. Stir in the red pepper flakes, parsley, and oregano and sauté for 1 minute. Increase the heat to medium-low and add the lobsters to the pan. Sauté on all sides, stirring often, until the shells turn red and the meat begins to become opaque. Add the tomatoes and salt, partially cover, and simmer gently until thickened, about 25 minutes. Remove from the heat and serve.

MUSSELS "PEPPETEDDA"

Serves 4

Here is another seafood recipe from Puglia, my father's home region on the Adriatic coast. *Peppetedda* means "peppery" in Pugliese dialect, referring to the hot paprika used. I tasted this dish when I traveled to Puglia for the first time to discover my paternal family's roots. Like most fare of the region, it is boldly flavored and simple in its execution. Remember to only buy mussels that are tightly closed.

6 POUNDS FRESH, MEDIUM-SIZE MUSSELS

4 TABLESPOONS EXTRA-VIRGIN OLIVE OIL

2 ONIONS, MINCED

3 LARGE CLOVES GARLIC, CUT INTO SMALL PIECES

3 TABLESPOONS CHOPPED FRESH FLAT-LEAF PARSLEY

2 TEASPOONS CHOPPED FRESH THYME, OR 1 TEASPOON DRIED THYME

1 BAY LEAF

1 CUP FRESH OR CANNED VINE-RIPENED TOMATOES, PEELED, CHOPPED, AND DRAINED

1 TEASPOON HOT PAPRIKA, OR 1 TEASPOON SWEET PAPRIKA AND GENEROUS PINCH RED PEPPER FLAKES

1½ CUPS GOOD-QUALITY DRY WHITE WINE

LOAF OF CRUSTY ARTISAN BREAD, SLICED

1. With a very stiff brush, scrub the mussels well. Pull or cut off their beards. Use a small sharp knife to scrape off any barnacles. Wash them under cold running water to remove any traces of sand. Place the mussels in a large bowl with enough cold water to cover to cleanse them of any sand, soaking for 1 to 3 hours. Rinse again, discarding any that open or whose shells are not very tightly shut.

2. In a heavy Dutch oven large enough to easily accommodate the mussels, warm the olive oil. Add the onion and garlic and sauté over medium heat until the onion wilts, about 4 minutes. Add the parsley, thyme, and bay leaf and continue to sauté for another few minutes until the onion is transparent. Add the tomatoes and the hot paprika or sweet paprika and red pepper flakes; simmer over medium heat until the sauce has thickened, about 7 minutes. Add the mussels, and using a wooden spoon, toss them with the sauce in the pan. Pour in the wine. Cover tightly and bring to a boil over medium-high heat. Lower the heat and simmer 2 to 3 minutes more, or until the mussels are fully open. Remove from the heat.

3. Discard any unopened mussels and divide the rest among 4 shallow bowls. Use a large spoon or ladle to spoon the mussel broth over each bowl, trying not to stir up the bottom, which may contain errant sand. Serve with plenty of bread.

9

FOR THE LOVE OF VEGETABLES:
VEGETARIAN MAIN COURSES AND
VEGETABLE SIDE DISHES

For many Italians, especially those south of Rome, eating meat had been a privilege of the wealthy until modern times. Grains, cheese, and vegetables have been the bedrock of their diet, and for good reasons. The climate is temperate, often with long growing seasons, and those staples keep well without refrigeration. Italy was slow to industrialize, which had two effects. It delayed the arrival of kitchen appliances taken for granted elsewhere and until the 1960s it kept much of the labor force under the *mezzadria* system (sharecropping) as *contadini,* or peasants on small, inefficient farms whose wealthy owners paid them not in cash but in kind: half the crop. Depending on "home-grown" thrift and caution, they developed a love for the land and its produce that is still strong. Italians still like to eat new peas in June and wild mushrooms in October, and open-air markets still thrive. They recognize such things as gifts from God and accord them almost religious veneration. In this chapter you will find recipes that offer a rich sampling of Italian vegetable specialties.

ZIA RITA'S
SMOTHERED CAULIFLOWER

Serves 4

Here is another of Zia Rita's inspired Italian recipes. The abundant quantity of delicious broth in this dish makes it imperative to serve the cauliflower with plenty of sturdy bread, which makes it a substantial side dish.

1 MEDIUM-SIZE HEAD CAULIFLOWER	SEA SALT TO TASTE
4 CLOVES GARLIC, CRUSHED	ZEST OF 1 LEMON
4 TABLESPOONS EXTRA-VIRGIN OLIVE OIL	FRESHLY GROUND BLACK PEPPER
1 BUNCH SCALLIONS, TRIMMED AND THINLY SLICED, INCLUDING 2 INCHES OF THE GREEN PART	1 SMALL BUNCH FLAT-LEAF PARSLEY, CHOPPED

1. Trim only the tough leaves off the cauliflower, leaving any of the tender green ones intact. Cut the bottom so that it sits straight in the pan. Using a small knife, make a crisscross at the base of the head to allow the cooking heat to permeate the stem.

2. Select a deep pan just the right size to fit the cauliflower and high enough to fit a cover over it. The pan should be neither too large nor too tight-fitting. Warm the garlic in the oil in the pan over medium-low heat until it colors nicely, about 3 minutes. Add the cauliflower and strew one-third of the sliced scallions, the salt, lemon zest, and plenty of pepper over it. Add 1 cup water. It should reach about halfway up the side of the cauliflower. Cover tightly and cook over medium heat for 5 minutes. Add the remaining scallions and 3 tablespoons of the parsley. Add up to 1 more cup of water if necessary to prevent the cauliflower from drying out. Simmer for 10 minutes, or until the water evaporates enough to form a rich, flavorful broth, and the bottom of the cauliflower is tender when pierced with a skewer into the center.

3. Bring the cauliflower to the table in a deep serving bowl in order to present it whole. Slice it at the table, cutting into wedges. Ladle some of the delicious broth over each portion and strew with the remaining parsley.

NONNA VERA'S
SWEET AND SOUR CARROTS
Serves 4

Vera Erenbourg D'Angara was a Russian painter and actress who was the first lady of the Russian theater in Geneva at the turn of the last century. After the Russian revolution, she lost her fabulous wealth within three days and in 1918 was taken stateless and penniless to Rome by Anna Maria D'Annunzio. She was a gifted cook, and her granddaughter, my friend Anna Maria Erenbourg Weld, has kindly shared her recipes. Many, such as this lovely sweet-and-sour dish, are a combination of Russian and Italian cooking (also see Nonna Vera's Tender and Crunchy Beef Medallions, page 133).

10 CARROTS	¼ CUP SUGAR
4 TABLESPOONS EXTRA-VIRGIN OLIVE OIL	½ TEASPOON SALT
3 TABLESPOONS UNSALTED BUTTER	2 TABLESPOONS RED WINE VINEGAR
2 ONIONS, THINLY SLICED	

1. Peel the carrots and cut off their tops. Slice them into ¼-inch rounds.

2. In a skillet, warm the olive oil and butter together. Add the onions and carrots and ½ cup water. Cover and allow the carrots to cook over medium heat until tender and the water is evaporated, stirring frequently, about 30 minutes. Sprinkle with the sugar, salt, and vinegar. Continue to cook, uncovered, until the carrots and onions become caramelized, crisp at the edges, and cast with a mahogany sheen. Serve at once.

SAUTÉED SWISS CHARD
WITH VINEGAR AND CRISPY BACON

Serves 4

Swiss chard and other greens are nourishing and good for the digestion. In southern Italy, they are a daily feature on the table. Lacinato (Tuscan) kale and collard greens can also be cooked this way. For a meatless version, omit the pancetta or bacon and substitute two or three additional tablespoons of olive oil.

¾ POUND SWISS CHARD

2 TABLESPOONS EXTRA-VIRGIN OLIVE OIL

3 OUNCES PANCETTA OR BACON, DICED

4 LARGE SHALLOTS, MINCED

½ TEASPOON SEA SALT

FRESHLY GROUND BLACK OR WHITE PEPPER

2 TABLESPOONS RED OR WHITE WINE VINEGAR, OR TO TASTE

1. Wash the chard well to dislodge any dirt clinging to the leaves. Drain any excess water but allow the water that clings to the leaves to remain. Use a sharp chef's knife to cut out the center rib and stem of every leaf. The easiest way to do this is to fold the leaf in half lengthwise and slice off the tough spine. Trim and discard the stems. Only if the stalks are tender, mince them. If they are tough, discard. Coarsely chop the greens.

2. In an ample nonreactive, nonstick casserole or Dutch oven, warm the olive oil. Add the pancetta or bacon to the pan and sauté over medium heat until crisp and browned, 4 to 5 minutes. Use a slotted spoon to transfer to a side dish. Discard all but 4 tablespoons of fat from the pan.

3. Add the shallots and minced stalks and sauté over medium-low heat until wilted, about 10 minutes. Add the greens to the pan and raise the heat to medium. Sauté, tossing occasionally, until the greens wilt completely but still retain their vivid color, about 5 minutes. Season with salt and pepper, sprinkle with the vinegar, and scatter with the pancetta or bacon. Serve hot.

TWO SIMPLE WAYS WITH
CABBAGE
Serve 6

In Italy, cabbage is cooked in many ways. The simplest is probably the Sardinian fashion of boiling cabbage in salted water until it is tender, and then sprinkling it with fruity olive oil (called *cauli a conca* in dialect). Even this elementary dish is delicious if the cabbage is young and fresh, and the oil full-bodied. It hardly seems necessary to write the method down for it. Another good, simple recipe is the way Anna Amendolara Nurse makes it, a version from Puglia. I especially like it with fennel seeds, but if serving it as an accompaniment with Moist Pan-Fried Pork Chops with Crunchy Crumb and Fennel Coating (page 126), substitute red pepper flakes.

2 TABLESPOONS EXTRA-VIRGIN OLIVE OIL

6 LARGE CLOVES GARLIC, SMASHED

3 OUNCES PANCETTA, DICED

RED PEPPER FLAKES TO TASTE, OR ½ TEASPOON FENNEL SEEDS

2½-POUND HEAD WHITE (STANDARD) CABBAGE, CORED AND SHREDDED

1 TEASPOON SEA SALT, OR TO TASTE

1. In a Dutch oven with a heavy bottom, warm the olive oil. Stir in the garlic and sauté until lightly colored, about 3 minutes. Remove and set aside.

2. Add the pancetta and the red pepper flakes or fennel seeds and sauté until golden, about 8 minutes. Stir in the cabbage and use a wooden spoon to toss well. Pour in ½ cup water and cover. Steam until thoroughly tender, about 30 minutes; if the cabbage begins to dry out or stick to the bottom of the pan, add up to ¼ cup more water.

3. Return the garlic to the cabbage if you like, add the salt, and serve.

WINTER SQUASH STEW
WITH TOMATO, DRY-CURED OLIVES, AND GARLIC

Serves 6

The combination of fresh pumpkin, sour black dry-cured olives, and tomatoes may sound unusual to Americans, but it is superb in this dish that I was raised on. Pumpkin or squash alone is bland, but the pungent dry-cured olives and garlic carry it to glory. Making this dish a day or two before you plan to serve it gives the flavors time to develop. Avoid serving it with other courses containing tomato sauce.

¼ CUP EXTRA-VIRGIN OLIVE OIL

3 LARGE CLOVES GARLIC, SLICED

1 CUP CANNED TOMATO SAUCE, OR ½ CUP TOMATO PASTE MIXED WITH ½ CUP WATER

1 MEDIUM-SIZE BUTTERNUT SQUASH OR 1 SMALL PUMPKIN (ABOUT 1½ POUNDS), PEELED, SEEDED, AND DICED

20 BLACK DRY-CURED MOROCCAN OLIVES, PITTED AND HALVED

1½ TEASPOONS CHOPPED FRESH THYME, OR ½ TEASPOON DRIED THYME

SEA SALT TO TASTE

FRESHLY GROUND BLACK PEPPER

1. In a saucepan over medium heat, warm the oil and garlic together until the garlic is fragrant, about 4 minutes. Add the tomato sauce, stir, and bring slowly to a simmer, about 4 minutes. Add the squash, olives, thyme, and ¾ cup water. Cover partially and simmer gently until tender, about 40 minutes.

2. Season with salt and pepper to taste. Serve immediately or chill and reheat gently before serving.

AHEAD-OF-TIME NOTE: This dish can be made up to 3 days in advance.

CASA JANCA'S
ROASTED PEPPERS

Serves 4

Cookbook writer Rosetta Costantino, author of *My Calabria,* offered this recipe from Casa Janca, a rustic *agriturismo* near the fishing village of Pizzo in Calabria. The owner, Rita Callipo, is a highly regarded cook who runs a restaurant out of her home. The peppers can be served as a vegetable side dish or as an appetizer, as they do in Calabria.

¼ CUP EXTRA-VIRGIN OLIVE OIL, PLUS MORE FOR GREASING

¼ CUP FRESHLY GRATED PECORINO CHEESE

½ CUP OF FRESH BREAD CRUMBS

1 LARGE CLOVE GARLIC, MINCED

2 TABLESPOONS FINELY CHOPPED FRESH FLAT-LEAF PARSLEY

4 MEDIUM-SIZE MIXED RED AND YELLOW BELL PEPPERS

SEA SALT

1 TABLESPOON CAPERS, CHOPPED IF USING LARGE CAPERS, OR CAPER BERRIES

6 ANCHOVY FILLETS, CUT IN SMALL PIECES

18 TO 20 SMALL CHERRY TOMATOES, CUT IN HALF OR QUARTERS IF LARGE

1. Preheat an oven to 400°F. Lightly oil a baking sheet or pan large enough to fit the peppers once they are cut into eight halves. In a small bowl, combine the grated cheese, bread crumbs, garlic, and parsley and mix well.

2. Cut the peppers in half lengthwise. Remove the stem and seeds. Place the peppers cut side up in the baking pan. Sprinkle with a little salt, the capers or caper berries, anchovy pieces, and cut-up tomatoes. Distribute the bread crumb mixture on top and drizzle each pepper half with the olive oil.

3. Slide the peppers onto the middle rack of the oven; bake until the peppers are thoroughly soft and nicely colored, about 45 minutes or longer, depending on the size of the peppers and their freshness.

4. Serve warm or at room temperature.

ANNA MARIA'S
ROASTED ONIONS WITH CRUMB TOPPING
Serves 4

Anna Maria Erenbourg Weld grew up in Rome watching her mother, grandmother, and great-grandmother cook. The three generations of women shopped and cooked daily for their extended family, which included eight relatives and the maid. Their cooking combined the traditions of both the Rome and Romagna branches of the matriarchy. This is one of their delicious vegetable dishes, suitable as a side dish or an appetizer.

6 TABLESPOONS EXTRA-VIRGIN OLIVE OIL

8 VIDALIA ONIONS (ABOUT 1½ POUNDS)

6 TABLESPOONS BREAD CRUMBS

1 TABLESPOON MINCED FRESH FLAT-LEAF PARSLEY

½ TEASPOON SEA SALT

FRESHLY GROUND BLACK PEPPER

1. Preheat an oven to 450°F. Grease 2 baking sheets well with the 6 tablespoons extra-virgin olive oil.

2. Peel the onions and cut them into horizontal slices ¼ inch thick. Transfer the slices to the baking sheets and slide them in the olive oil on both sides to coat evenly and distribute the oil evenly in the pan at the same time.

3. In a small bowl, combine the bread crumbs, parsley, salt, and pepper to taste. Sprinkle the bread crumb mixture evenly over each of the onion slices. Distribute a total of 12 tablespoons water around the slices in both baking sheets. Slide onto the middle and upper racks of the oven and bake until the onions are tender and almost transparent within and browned and crunchy on the surface, about 20 minutes. Serve hot or at room temperature, as preferred.

CREAMY MASHED POTATOES
WITH GARLIC

Serves 4

In the Italian fashion of making mashed potatoes, the cooked potatoes are mashed, then returned to the pan and whipped slowly as butter, followed by hot milk, are beaten into them until they are creamy, light, and fluffy. These pureed potatoes are indispensable with many of the meat dishes in this book. You can include the garlic or not. In this version, abundant garlic is boiled with the potatoes until it is soft and creamy, and the lot is later mashed together.

1½ POUNDS MATURE BOILING POTATOES OR YUKON GOLD POTATOES

12 LARGE CLOVES GARLIC, SKINS ON

4 TABLESPOONS (½ STICK) UNSALTED BUTTER, CUT INTO THIN SLICES

SEA SALT

¾ CUP HOT MILK

FRESHLY GROUND WHITE PEPPER

1. Reject any potatoes that are green, or cut off any green parts. Scrub the potatoes well but leave their skins on.

2. Place the potatoes in a pot with enough cold water to cover. Partially cover the pot and bring to a boil over high heat. Reduce the heat to medium and continue to cook until the potatoes are tender, about 30 minutes. Drop the garlic cloves in the water 15 minutes before the potatoes are done. Test for doneness by inserting a cake tester or a sharp knife into the potatoes and garlic.

3. Drain the potatoes and garlic and allow them to cool just until they are comfortable to handle. Rinse the pot. Peel the potatoes and the garlic and pass them through a potato ricer back into the pot. (In a potato ricer, the potatoes are forced through small holes, with the result that there will be no lumps in the mashed potatoes.) If a potato ricer is not available, transfer the peeled potatoes and garlic to the pot and use a potato masher to thoroughly mash them and press out any lumps.

4. Place the pot over a flame-tamer, if available. Alternatively, place the pot over the lowest possible heat and stir constantly as you work to prevent the potatoes on the bottom of the pan from becoming scorched. Add the butter, and salt to taste. Use an electric beater if available, or a whisk, to beat the potatoes while pouring in the hot milk a little at a time. The potatoes will become light and creamy.

5. Remove the pot from the heat. Adjust for salt and add pepper to taste, beating with the beater or whisk. Serve immediately.

POTATOES SCHISCIONERA
Serves 6

Another of my aunt's infallible Sardinian recipes, these potatoes are stewed slowly with garlic and parsley, which makes them moist, creamy, and very flavorful. This is a lovely side dish with Whole Roasted Chicken with Garlic, Fresh Garden Herbs, and Pan Gravy (page 112), Luisa Petruccci's Oven-Fried Chicken with Bread Crumbs (page 120), Nonna Vera's Tender and Crunchy Beef Medallions (page 133), or Juicy Meat Loaf with Tomato and Red Wine Glaze (page 136).

2 TABLESPOONS EXTRA-VIRGIN OLIVE OIL

2 LARGE CLOVES GARLIC, FINELY CHOPPED OR GRATED

5 MEDIUM-SIZE BOILING POTATOES (ABOUT 1½ POUNDS), PEELED AND CUT INTO 1-INCH CUBES

SEA SALT TO TASTE

FRESHLY GROUND BLACK PEPPER

2 TABLESPOONS CHOPPED FRESH FLAT-LEAF PARSLEY

Place the oil and garlic in a cold saucepan large enough to accommodate the potatoes later. Turn on the heat to low and sauté until the garlic is softened, about 2 minutes. Add the potatoes and stir. Add 1 cup water, the salt, pepper to taste, and the parsley. Cover and simmer over medium heat until the potatoes are tender, about 20 minutes, stirring occasionally as they cook to prevent them from sticking to the pan. Serve.

AHEAD-OF-TIME NOTE: This dish can be made up to 2 days in advance, then cooled, covered, and refrigerated. Reheat gently over low heat.

VIOLA BUITONI'S
SAUTÉED BROCCOLI RAPINI WITH POTATOES

Serves 4

America has at last discovered this wonderful vegetable (often called "raab" in English), but I'm convinced that people would like it more if it they had it prepared correctly. The secret to cooking broccoli *rapini* is to boil the greens briefly before sautéing, to rid them of their excessive bitterness and to tenderize the stalks.

2 YUKON GOLD POTATOES, UNPEELED

1 BUNCH BROCCOLI RABE, ABOUT 1½ POUNDS

1 TABLESPOON SEA SALT

5 TABLESPOONS EXTRA-VIRGIN OLIVE OIL

6 LARGE CLOVES GARLIC, BRUISED BUT LEFT WHOLE

1. In a saucepan, combine the potatoes with enough cold water to cover and bring to a boil. Cook over medium heat until the potatoes are tender, about 20 minutes. They should be fully tender but not falling apart when cooked. When cool enough to handle, peel the skin from the potatoes, cut them lengthwise into quarters, and then cut crosswise into medium-thin slices. Set aside.

2. Using a small, sharp knife, peel the skin from the tough lower stalks of the *rapini* (most of the bottom portion of the stalk) and cut them crosswise into 3-inch lengths. Fill a large pot with plenty of water to cover the greens and bring to a rolling boil. Add the greens along with the salt, cover partially, and cook until the stalks are completely tender but not mushy, about 5 minutes after the water returns to a boil. Note that if the stalks are at all crisp, they will remain bitter. Drain the greens, reserving a little of the cooking liquid. Set aside separately.

3. In a nonstick skillet large enough to accommodate the potatoes and the greens, warm 3 tablespoons of the olive oil and add the garlic. Sauté over medium heat until the garlic is nicely softened but not colored, about 4 minutes. Transfer to a side dish. Raise the heat to medium-high and add the potatoes. Sauté until they are golden and crispy all over, about 12 minutes, then transfer to another side dish. Warm the remaining 2 tablespoons olive oil over medium heat, then return the *rapini* and the garlic cloves to the pan. Sauté until the greens are nicely coated with the olive oil and the garlic and heated through, about 3 minutes; if they appear a little dry, add a little of the reserved cooking water as needed. Return the potatoes to the skillet and toss all together. Adjust for seasoning and serve immediately.

10

SUNDAY TREATS:
FRUIT DESSERTS, SWEETS, AND CONFECTIONS

Innumerable *pasticcerie,* or pastry shops, offer the fine and fancy year-round while home cooks produce uncomplicated, homespun desserts that often—like so much else in the Italian kitchen—appear according to season or occasion (engagements, weddings, religious feasts, or festivals). Sweet yeast breads enriched with almonds or candied fruit are typical, and there are countless sugar-dusted fritters along the lines of *zeppole,* and of course *biscotti* (which means, literally, "twice cooked"). There are specialties that are only made on particular religious holidays or festivities, or that are traditional for engagements, *carnevale,* or other significant occasions. The "love knots" recipe in this chapter is my grandmother's. My father craved these Pugliese cookies, which his sister baked for him every year on his birthday until he died at the age of 100. Such desserts are as versatile as they are uncomplicated and homespun. Italians serve them at breakfast, as snacks, and after dinner.

BAKED APPLES WITH GRENADINE

Serves 4

Another of my friend Anna Amendolara's comforting home recipes, these baked apples are delicious with cream or vanilla ice cream. Grenadine, the prominent flavoring, is pomegranate syrup. You can find it in your supermarket, usually in the section where cocktail mixes are sold. Rome apples are the best variety to use for baking because they keep their shape when cooked.

4 LARGE APPLES, PREFERABLY ROME

4 TEASPOONS SUGAR

1 TEASPOON CINNAMON

¾ CUP GRENADINE SYRUP

HEAVY CREAM OR VANILLA ICE CREAM, FOR SERVING

1. Preheat an oven to 375°F.

2. Remove the stems and cut out the blossom ends of the apples. Do not core through but peel one third down from the top. Place in a baking pan large enough to accommodate all the apples without touching. Sprinkle with the sugar and cinnamon. Pour grenadine over each apple. Add ⅔ cup water to the pan and bake, uncovered, until soft, 45 minutes.

3. Serve warm or cold, with cream or vanilla ice cream.

ORANGE-ALMOND RING CAKE
WITH ORANGE GLAZE

Serves 8 to 10

I learned this lovely recipe from my friend, baker and food writer Susan G. Purdy, who discovered this moist cake bursting with citrus flavor in a seaside restaurant in Liguria. It has a slightly crunchy texture due to the ground almonds, but the predominant flavor is orange, enhanced by flecks of bright zest and an orange glaze. If you prefer a stronger almond flavor, you can substitute almond extract for the orange or use half almond and half orange.

SOLID VEGETABLE SHORTENING OR UNSALTED BUTTER, FOR GREASING

1¼ CUPS SIFTED ALL-PURPOSE FLOUR, PLUS MORE FOR DUSTING

1¼ CUPS (6 OUNCES) WHOLE OR SLIVERED ALMONDS (BLANCHED OR WITH SKINS)

1½ CUPS GRANULATED SUGAR, DIVIDED

2½ TEASPOONS BAKING POWDER

¾ TEASPOON SEA SALT

3 LARGE EGGS, SEPARATED, PLUS 2 WHOLE LARGE EGGS, AT ROOM TEMPERATURE

¼ TEASPOON CREAM OF TARTAR

½ CUP GRAPE SEED OIL OR VEGETABLE OIL

4 TEASPOONS GRATED ORANGE ZEST

1 TABLESPOON EXTRA-FINE JULIENNED ORANGE ZEST (FROM 2 LARGE NAVEL ORANGES)

1¾ TEASPOONS PURE ORANGE EXTRACT

¾ CUP FRESHLY SQUEEZED ORANGE JUICE WITH PULP, AT ROOM TEMPERATURE

FOR THE GLAZE

1½ CUPS SIFTED CONFECTIONERS' SUGAR

1 TABLESPOON GRATED ORANGE ZEST, PLUS THE JUICE OF 1 ORANGE AT ROOM TEMPERATURE

1 TEASPOON FRESHLY SQUEEZED LEMON JUICE, AT ROOM TEMPERATURE

EQUIPMENT

10-INCH BUNDT OR TUBE PAN

1. Preheat the oven to 350°F. Generously coat the inside of a 10-inch Bundt or tube pan with the shortening or butter, then dust with flour; tap out excess flour.

2. In a food processor fitted with a steel blade, combine the almonds with ¼ cup of the granulated sugar. Pulse until the almonds are finely ground, 1 to 2 minutes, then turn them out into a bowl. In another bowl, whisk together the flour, baking powder, and salt, then whisk into the almonds.

3. In the large bowl of an electric mixer, combine 3 egg whites and the cream of tartar; reserve the yolks in a separate bowl. Whip until the whites are foamy, then continue to whip on medium speed while slowly adding ¾ cup of the sugar. Whip until soft peaks form, then transfer to a clean bowl.

4. In the previously used mixer bowl, combine the reserved yolks plus 2 extra whole eggs, the oil, the remaining ½ cup of the sugar, both the grated and

julienned orange zest, and the orange extract. Beat on high for about 2 minutes, until pale in color. With the mixer on low speed, add the orange juice and beat for another minute. Remove the bowl from the mixer stand. By hand, fold in the flour-almond mixture, then the egg whites, in three separate additions, to lighten the batter.

5. Scoop the batter into the prepared pan, smooth the top, and bake on the middle rack of the oven for 35 to 40 minutes, or until a cake tester inserted in the center comes out clean. Cool the cake in its pan on a wire rack for at least 20 minutes. Invert the cake onto a rack or plate and cool completely.

6. While the cake is cooling, prepare the glaze. In a small bowl, whisk together the confectioners' sugar, the orange juice, and the lemon juice until smooth and slightly runny. Drizzle the glaze over the cooled cake and sprinkle the grated orange zest over the top.

SUNDAY TREATS: FRUIT DESSERTS, SWEETS, AND CONFECTIONS

NONNA CLIA'S
APPLE CAKE

Serves 6

The recipe for this typical Italian cake is kindly offered by my friend Flavia Destefanis. She writes, "My maternal grandmother, Clia, who loved her country house in Montepulciano, near Siena, would whip this up for an afternoon tea. Egg size always depended on the whim of the chicken in our chicken coop. Quantities were never set in stone, nor were the ingredients: sometimes she added the zest of a lemon and no vanilla, sometimes she would throw in a few walnuts if she had the inkling. Any flaws that might show up were covered up by the dusting of sugar." This cake can be made with other types of fruit that are in season, such as plums, washed, dried, and quartered, or apricots, or a combination of apples and pears. Just add a bit more flour if the fruit is quite wet.

SOLID VEGETABLE SHORTENING OR BUTTER, FOR GREASING

3 LARGE EGGS

5 TABLESPOONS GRANULATED SUGAR

1 TEASPOON PURE VANILLA EXTRACT

10 TABLESPOONS (1¼ STICKS) UNSALTED BUTTER, MELTED AND COOLED

1¼ CUPS UNBLEACHED ALL-PURPOSE FLOUR, PLUS MORE FOR DUSTING

1 TEASPOON BAKING POWDER

1 TEASPOON BAKING SODA

⅛ TEASPOON SALT

4 MEDIUM-SIZE APPLES, PEELED, CORED, AND CUT INTO ¾-INCH CUBES

CONFECTIONERS' SUGAR, FOR DUSTING

EQUIPMENT

9-INCH SPRINGFORM PAN, PREFERABLY, BUT ANY PAN WILL DO

1. Preheat the oven to 375°F. Select a 9-inch springform cake pan with sides that are at least 2 inches high. Generously grease the pan with solid vegetable shortening or butter and dust with flour. Tap out the excess flour and set aside.

2. In a mixing bowl, beat the eggs. Whisk in the granulated sugar and vanilla until blended, about 45 seconds. Stir in the butter. Sift in the flour, baking powder, baking soda, and salt until just combined to form a thick, sticky batter. Additional flour may be necessary, depending on the size of the eggs. Fold in the apple cubes and transfer the batter to the prepared pan.

3. Bake until golden brown and a toothpick inserted into the center comes out clean, 35 to 40 minutes. Cool on a wire rack for at least 20 minutes, then run a paring knife around the sides of the pan to loosen. Place a wire rack over the pan and invert the pan and wire rack together. Lift off the cake pan and let the cake cool right side up for 20 minutes, then transfer to a serving platter. Dust the surface with confectioners' sugar. Cut into wedges, and serve.

AUNT NETTIE'S
ITALIAN CHEESECAKE
Serves 8 to 10

My aunt and godmother, Annette Messina, was a superb baker and she was famous for this ricotta cheesecake. The crust is a classic *pasta frolla,* a sweet, cookie-like dough. As with most cheesecakes, this tart must be aged to develop its flavor. It should be made at least a day in advance, and is best eaten within 2 or 3 days of baking, but it will keep up to 1 week, chilled.

FOR THE CRUST:

2 CUPS SIFTED PASTRY FLOUR OR UNBLEACHED ALL-PURPOSE FLOUR

½ CUP GRANULATED SUGAR

PINCH OF SALT

8 TABLESPOONS (1 STICK) COLD UNSALTED BUTTER, PLUS MORE FOR GREASING

1 LARGE EGG, BEATEN WITH 1 TABLESPOON MILK

FOR THE FILLING

2½ CUPS DRAINED FRESH WHOLE-MILK RICOTTA

8 OUNCES MASCARPONE CHEESE, AT ROOM TEMPERATURE

¾ CUP PLUS 2 TABLESPOONS SUGAR

⅓ CUP ALL-PURPOSE UNBLEACHED FLOUR

4 EXTRA-LARGE EGGS

¼ CUP RUM

¼ CUP CHOPPED BITTERSWEET CHOCOLATE

¼ CUP CHOPPED CANDIED ORANGE RIND

½ TEASPOON GROUND CINNAMON

GRATED ZEST OF 1 ORANGE

GRATED ZEST OF 1 LEMON

1 CUP HEAVY CREAM

CONFECTIONERS' SUGAR, FOR DUSTING

EQUIPMENT

8-INCH SPRINGFORM PAN

1. First make the crust: Sift the flour, granulated sugar, and salt together into a medium bowl. Using a pastry cutter or 2 dinner knives, cut in the butter until a crumb-like mixture is formed. Using a fork, mix the beaten egg into the flour mixture until evenly moistened. Using your hands, gather about two-thirds of the dough into a ball and the remaining one-third into a second ball. Wrap each ball separately in plastic wrap and refrigerate for 1 hour or overnight before using.

2. Generously butter an 8-inch springform pan. Preheat the oven to 350°F. Sprinkle a work surface lightly with flour and roll the larger ball of dough into a disk ⅛ inch thick. Crimp aluminum foil under and around the sides of the pan to catch any leaks during baking. Fit the crust into the pan and crimp the edges. Roll out the second ball of dough into a disk ⅛ inch thick. Cut it into strips about ½ inch wide. Refrigerate the dough-lined pan and the strips of dough until ready for use.

3. To make the filling, beat the ricotta and mascarpone together in a large bowl until well blended. Stir in the ¾ cup granulated sugar and the flour. Beat in one egg at a

time until each is fully incorporated into the mixture. Stir in the rum, chocolate, candied rind, cinnamon, and zests, and blend thoroughly.

4. In a deep bowl, beat the heavy cream with the 2 tablespoons sugar until soft peaks form. Fold into the ricotta mixture until blended. Pour the ricotta filling into the prepared pan and smooth the top evenly. Arrange the strips of dough in a diagonal lattice over the filling, trim where necessary, and pinch onto the crust. Slide the pan onto the middle rack of the oven and bake until a skewer inserted into the center of the cake comes out clean, 1 hour to 1 hour and 15 minutes. Turn off the oven and leave the cake inside with the door closed for about 1 hour. Take out and cool completely. Remove the sides of the springform pan. Slide the cake onto a cake platter, cover with plastic wrap, and refrigerate overnight before serving.

5. Before serving, dust the cheesecake with confectioners' sugar. The cheesecake is usually cut it into small slices and accompanied with espresso.

AUNT NETTIE'S
SWEET LOVE KNOTS
Makes 8 to 9 Dozen

The recipe for this traditional cookie, *taralli dolci*, of the Puglia region came from my paternal grandmother but my aunt, a talented baker, fiddled with the original recipe whenever she made it until her *taralli* were the best and the lightest I've ever had. This is how she does it.

5 CUPS UNSIFTED FLOUR, PLUS ADDITIONAL

1½ CUPS GRANULATED SUGAR (1¼ IF YOU LIKE IT LESS SWEET)

6 TEASPOONS BAKING POWDER

16 TABLESPOONS (2 STICKS) UNSALTED BUTTER, AT ROOM TEMPERATURE

8 EXTRA-LARGE EGGS

3 TABLESPOONS PURE VANILLA EXTRACT

FOR THE GLAZE

1½ CUPS CONFECTIONERS' SUGAR

½ CUP WATER OR MILK

1. Preheat the oven to 350°F.

2. In a mixing bowl, combine the flour, granulated sugar, and baking powder. Cut the butter into the flour mixture as if making pie crust. If mixing by hand, make a "well" in the center of the mixture.

3. Beat the eggs with the vanilla and pour them into the well. Gradually add the flour into the eggs until it is all incorporated. Wash hands well and mix and knead the dough until smooth. You may have to add more flour until the dough is soft but workable. Turn the dough out onto a clean, lightly floured work surface. Keep adding a little flour to the surface, as necessary, as you are shaping the dough if it sticks.

4. To form the cookies, take a piece of dough the size of a walnut and roll it with your hands on the work surface to form a log about the size of your middle finger. Then take one end of the log and place it over the opposite end so that a small hole remains in the center. Place the "love knots" on cookie sheets about 1 inch apart. Bake until lightly browned, about 18 minutes.

5. While the cookies are baking, make the glaze. In a medium bowl, whisk the confectioners' sugar with the water until smooth. While the cookies are cooling, brush the tops with the glaze; it should have a thick consistency, as it will melt on the surface and form a thick glaze as the *taralli* cool.

SWEET EASTER BREAD

Makes 2 loaves

This delicious, delicate sweet bread is traditional in many Italian homes on Easter morning with boiled eggs to symbolize rebirth, along with a platter of *salumi*. The sweet bread resembles panettone, but is less buttery. One of the many variations of this bread relies on cinnamon for flavoring, which may be included here if you like. Others include the addition of golden raisins or diced candied fruit. The recipe should be started early in the day, as some five or six hours are necessary for it to rise. It is better to use a heavy-duty electric mixer than to work by hand, as the dough requires extensive kneading before the first rise.

FOR THE SPONGE

½ CUP WARM MILK (105 TO 115°F) OR LUKEWARM MILK (80° TO 90°F)

1½ PACKAGES (3½ TEASPOONS) ACTIVE DRY YEAST, OR 1½ CAKES COMPRESSED YEAST

½ CUP BREAD FLOUR

FOR THE DOUGH

SPONGE, AS ABOVE

10 EXTRA-LARGE EGG YOLKS AT ROOM TEMPERATURE

SCANT ⅔ CUP GRANULATED SUGAR

9 TABLESPOONS UNSALTED BUTTER, AT ROOM TEMPERATURE, PLUS MORE FOR GREASING

½ CUP MILK

GRATED ZEST OF 4 LEMONS

2 TEASPOONS PURE VANILLA EXTRACT

2 TABLESPOONS ROSE WATER

2 TEASPOONS GROUND CINNAMON (OPTIONAL)

3⅓ CUPS BREAD FLOUR

1 EXTRA-LARGE EGG WHITE, LIGHTLY BEATEN

CONFECTIONERS' SUGAR, FOR DUSTING

1. In the bowl of an electric mixer, stir the warm milk and dry yeast together until dissolved. Leave until foamy, about 12 minutes. Stir in the flour. Cover tightly with plastic wrap and let rest until doubled in bulk and spongy in texture, about 1 hour.

2. To make the dough, fit the mixer with the paddle attachment and attach the bowl with the sponge. With the machine running, add the egg yolks, one at a time. Add the granulated sugar and beat until creamy, then gradually add the butter, milk, lemon zest, vanilla, rose water, cinnamon (if using), and flour. Beat on medium for at least 12 minutes, stopping occasionally to scrape down the sides, until the dough is barely sticky. Cover tightly with plastic wrap, then with a clean kitchen towel. Let rise in a warm, draft-free place until tripled in bulk, about 3 hours.

3. Generously butter 2 9 x 5-inch loaf pans. Punch the dough down and turn it out onto a floured work surface. Grease your hands with butter or olive oil and knead the dough to work out the large bubbles, about 5 minutes. It should remain very

soft, almost sticky, and elastic. Divide the dough in half and place each half in one of the buttered loaf pans. Cover the pans tightly with plastic wrap and cover with kitchen towels. Let rise once again until the dough doubles in bulk, about 2½ hours.

4. Preheat the oven to 375°F. Brush the surface of each loaf with the egg white and slide the pans onto the middle rack of the oven. Bake until golden, about 12 minutes. Cover loosely with aluminum foil and bake about 20 minutes longer, until the top of the loaves balloon into a great dome and are golden brown. Remove and let cool for about 5 minutes, then carefully transfer to wire racks to cool. When the loaves are completely cool, dust generously with confectioners' sugar.

NONNA MESSINA'S
ITALIAN SESAME SEED COOKIES
Makes 8 Dozen

My aunt learned to make many Sicilian sweets from her Sicilian mother-in-law, Santa Messina, a widow who devoted her life to cooking and baking for her sons. These classic cookies, while simple, turned up at festivities and on holidays, but they are terrific at breakfast for dunking into espresso or coffee. They will keep up to 3 months or more in a closed container placed in a cool, dry place. If using a food processor, you will need to halve the recipe.

4 CUPS UNBLEACHED ALL-PURPOSE FLOUR

1½ CUPS SUGAR

1 TABLESPOON BAKING POWDER

½ TEASPOON SALT

6 TABLESPOONS UNSALTED BUTTER

2 LARGE EGGS, LIGHTLY BEATEN

½ CUP MILK, PLUS ¼ CUP FOR BRUSHING

1 TEASPOON PURE VANILLA EXTRACT

2 CUPS UNSALTED SESAME SEEDS (TOASTED OR UNTOASTED)

1. Sift the dry ingredients into a mixing bowl. Cut in the butter with two knives or a cookie cutter until it resembles coarse meal.

2. Combine the eggs, milk, and vanilla and stir them into the dry ingredients to make a soft dough. Chill the dough for 1 hour.

3. Preheat the oven to 375°F. Line two baking sheets with parchment paper.

4. Form the dough into "ropes" about 2½ inches long and ½ inch in diameter. Brush the pieces with milk and roll them in the sesame seeds until they are well covered. Place 1 inch apart on the baking sheets and bake for 20 to 25 minutes, or until golden. Remove from the oven and transfer to racks to cool.

FRAPPE

Serves 6

These addictive Italian pastry fritters are inescapable in the repertoire of Italian sweets, and there are many names for them. My mother called them *frappe* and my paternal grandmother called them *cartedatte*. My mother's were lighter, but my grandmother Domenica made a beautiful syrup for dunking or pouring over them (see opposite). The best pastries of this genre are very crisp and so delicately thin that they are in essence *vaporoso,* "like vapor," as the Italians sometimes say. It is better if the dough incorporates grappa, wine, or some kind of liquor, as it causes the pastries to fry up crisp and makes them light. Another rule is to roll out the dough as thin as possible. I always use a hand-cranked pasta machine, passing the dough through the rollers set on the last notch. *Frappe* can be eaten right after they are cooked, or up to a couple of weeks afterward if stored in tightly sealed tins at room temperature to ensure their crispness.

GENEROUS 2 CUPS UNBLEACHED ALL-PURPOSE FLOUR, OR AS NEEDED

2 TABLESPOONS COLD UNSALTED BUTTER, CUT INTO SMALL PIECES

3 EXTRA-LARGE EGGS AT ROOM TEMPERATURE

3 TABLESPOONS GRANULATED SUGAR

¼ TEASPOON SALT

¼ CUP DRY VERMOUTH, DRY SHERRY, GRAPPA, OR RUM

CORN OIL, FOR DEEP-FRYING

CONFECTIONERS' SUGAR, FOR DUSTING

1. To make by hand, sift the flour into a bowl. Add the butter pieces and, using your fingers or a pastry blender, work them in until the mixture is the consistency of coarse meal. Turn the mixture out onto a work surface. Using your fingers, make a well in the center of the mound.

2. In a bowl, stir together the eggs, granulated sugar, salt, and wine or grappa with a fork until blended. Pour the mixture into the well and, using the fork and always stirring in the same direction, draw the dry ingredients into the wet ingredients. When a pliable dough begins to form, set the fork aside and work with your hands. If too soft, sprinkle in flour a little at a time—but the dough shouldn't be too stiff.

3. To make in a food processor, put the flour and butter into the bowl and process until the butter becomes crumb-like, about 30 seconds. Add the eggs, granulated sugar, salt, and wine or grappa and process until a smooth dough forms.

4. Divide the dough into 4 equal portions. Work with 1 portion at a time, keeping the other portions covered with a clean, slightly damp kitchen towel. On a floured work surface, use a rolling pin to roll out the dough paper-thin—the thinner, the

better. Alternatively, divide the dough into 8 equal portions, and roll out each portion into the thinnest strip possible on a hand-cranked pasta machine: Start out at the widest setting and pass the dough through each consecutive setting once, ending with the last setting. If the dough sticks, dust it lightly with flour before passing it through the rollers.

5. Cut the dough strip into rectangles about 2 by 3 inches. Make a horizontal cut in the center of each rectangle; this helps them fry evenly. Spread the rectangles out on clean, dry kitchen towels. Cover them with more clean, dry kitchen towels. Roll out and cut the remaining dough portions in the same way.

6. Pour the corn oil into a deep skillet to a depth of 2 inches and heat over high heat until a scrap of dough sizzles upon contact. Add the dough rectangles, a few at a time, but do not crowd the pan. There should be enough oil around each rectangle to allow quick and even cooking. Fry, turning once, until evenly golden on both sides, about 2 minutes. Adjust the heat if the pastries are browning too quickly. Using a wire skimmer, transfer to paper towels to drain. You can stack them, but put paper towels between the layers to absorb the excess oil. When all of the pastries are fried, let cool completely, then dust generously with confectioners' sugar.

NONNA DOMENICA'S
RAISIN SAUCE WITH PORT WINE

Makes 2¼ cups

The irresistible aroma of fruit, port, and cinnamon as this sauce bubbles on the stovetop always reminds me of the holidays. The original recipe called for *vin santo*, which is difficult to find outside of Italy, but I find that port wine works splendidly. Serve alongside rice, noodle, or bread puddings, or with the *frappe* as a dipping sauce.

1 POUND RAISINS	PINCH OF FRESHLY GRATED NUTMEG
1 CUP PORT WINE	1 CINNAMON STICK
½ TEASPOON CLOVES	½ CUP HONEY

1. In a medium saucepan, bring the raisins in 3 cups of water to a boil. Cover the pan, lower the heat to a simmer, and cook for 1 hour. Strain the raisins through a food mill. You should have approximately 2 cups of syrup.

2. Return the syrup to the pan and add the port, cloves, nutmeg, cinnamon, and honey. Simmer for another 30 minutes. Let cool before using.

VENETIAN PUDDING
WITH CUSTARD SAUCE

Serves 6 to 8

I adapted this recipe for fragrant bread pudding from an old Venetian dessert designed for using up stale bread. It is light and delicate due in part to the fact that the "stale" bread is finely shredded before it soaks in the milk. Ginger, orange zest, cinnamon, and mace enhance it with their beguiling flavors and scents. I like to serve custard sauce with it, but offer it with whipped cream instead, if you prefer. Note: The easiest way to grate fresh ginger is to peel it when it is fresh and freeze it until ready to use; it grates very easily when it is frozen solid.

1 POUND CRUST-FREE, STALE CHALLAH-STYLE BREAD (ABOUT 1¼ POUNDS WITH CRUST)

4 CUPS MILK

⅓ CUP ALMONDS, GROUND

½ CUP WALNUTS, GROUND

⅔ CUP GOLDEN RAISINS

1 TABLESPOON FRESHLY GRATED ZEST OF 1 LARGE NAVEL ORANGE

1 TABLESPOON GRATED FRESH GINGER

7 TABLESPOONS SUGAR

2 TABLESPOONS HONEY

½ TEASPOON GROUND MACE

1 TEASPOON GROUND CINNAMON

¼ TEASPOON SEA SALT

5 EXTRA-LARGE EGGS, SEPARATED

UNSALTED BUTTER, FOR GREASING

¼ CUP FINE, FRESH WHITE BREAD CRUMBS, FOR COATING

FOR THE CUSTARD SAUCE

5 TEASPOONS SUGAR

1 EGG YOLK

1 HEAPING TABLESPOON CORNSTARCH

1 CUP MILK

SMALL PINCH OF SALT

1-INCH STRIP OF LEMON ZEST

1. Preheat the oven to 375°F.

2. Using your fingers, tear the bread into thin shreds. In a large bowl, combine the shredded bread and the milk and let soak for 10 to 15 minutes. Toss occasionally to ensure even soaking. Mix in the ground nuts, golden raisins, orange zest, ginger, sugar, honey, mace, cinnamon, and salt.

3. In a separate bowl, beat the egg yolks until light yellow and blended. Add to the bread mixture and blend. In yet another bowl, using an electric mixer, beat the egg whites until they begin to form peaks easily, but are not so stiff that they begin to separate into liquid and solid parts. Using a large rubber or plastic spatula, gently fold the whites into the bread mixture just until no white streaks remain.

4. Select a wide, shallow baking pan about 9 x 13 x 2 inches. If it is too deep, the pudding will be too moist in the center. Grease the pan generously with butter.

Sprinkle the bread crumbs into the pan evenly, then tilt the pan to coat the entire surface with a uniform layer. Tap out any excess. Pour the batter into the prepared baking dish, taking care not to disturb the coating on the pan and smoothing the surface to ensure an equal depth throughout. Bake until nicely golden brown, about 40 minutes. Turn off the oven and let the pudding rest in the oven for another 10 to 15 minutes. Remove the pan from the oven and let the pudding cool completely on a rack.

5. While the bread pudding is cooling, make the custard sauce. In a saucepan, add the sugar to the egg yolk and beat with a whisk for a few minutes until creamy. Add the cornstarch, beating to incorporate. Add 2 tablespoons of the milk, using a wooden spoon to make a creamy mixture. Add the salt and lemon zest to the rest of the milk. Place the pan over low heat and gradually add the rest of the milk mixture. Stir constantly until the mixture begins to simmer gently and thickens enough to coat a spoon. Remove from the stove, cover, and keep warm.

6. Cut the bread pudding into squares or rectangles, as desired. Place a tablespoon or two of the warm custard on individual serving plates. Lay a portion of the pudding over the custard and serve.

BABY'S FIRST FOOD
(GROWN-UPS LOVE IT TOO)

Italians eat well as adults because they ate well as children. They grew up on wholesome food, the food their elders ate, not baby food or toddler's food or sugar-, fat-, or salt-laden stuff made in factories, processed with chemicals for long, perhaps eternal shelf-life and enhanced profit margins. Italian parents are attentive to nutritious, natural food, made always from the freshest and finest ingredients, and not only in their homes. It is not unusual to see an Italian youngster in a restaurant, being tutored on the fine points of good eating by his parents and even by the waiters. There are recipes in this chapter for comforting foods Italian children grow up with. I chose them because they are quick to prepare and are nourishing, but they are no less appealing to adults.

ALPHABET AND VEGETABLE SOUP
WITH MOZZARELLA DICE

Serves 4 children

Children have fun fishing for pasta alphabets in their soup and then eating them. When I was a child in the 1950s, the closest my American schoolmates got to this traditional childhood classic was canned alphabet soup—and they loved it. The nutritious homemade version (the corn is a recent addition) is better, I promise—and you won't have any trouble getting little ones to eat it. If you like, drop in diced mozzarella or "string cheese" before serving, as my mother often did; children love the oozy strings of cheese as it melts in the hot broth.

1 FRESH EAR OF CORN	1 SMALL ZUCCHINI, FINELY DICED
1 LEAF SWISS CHARD	1 SMALL ONION OR 1 SHALLOT, FINELY DICED
4 CUPS VEGETABLE BROTH (PAGE 215) OR CHICKEN BROTH (PAGE 214)	1 TEASPOON SEA SALT, OR TO TASTE
1 SMALL CELERY STALK, INCLUDING LEAVES, STRINGS REMOVED, FINELY DICED	¼ CUP ALPHABET PASTINA
1 SMALL CARROT, FINELY DICED	¼ CUP MOZZARELLA OR "STRING CHEESE," FINELY DICED (OPTIONAL)
1 FRESH OR CANNED PLUM TOMATO, PEELED, SEEDED, AND CHOPPED	

1. Slice the kernels off the ear of corn. Cut the thick rib off the chard and mince it. Chop the leafy part and set all aside.

2. Pour the broth in a soup pot and stir in the celery, chard, carrot, and tomato. Simmer, partially covered, until they are tender, about 20 minutes. Add the corn, zucchini, onion or shallot, salt, and alphabet pastina and simmer for another 5 minutes, or less, until the pastina is cooked to your liking. If adding the cheese, drop it into each individual bowl. Serve.

SEMOLINA
IN BROTH

Serves 4 children or 3 adults

This is a smooth, comforting soup that children love. You can buy coarsely ground semolina, which resembles grits or polenta meal, in health food stores and some Italian specialty shops, or substitute farina hot cereal, which is the same thing—as long as it is not the instant variety.

2 TABLESPOONS EXTRA-VIRGIN OLIVE OIL OR UNSALTED BUTTER	1 QUART CHICKEN BROTH (PAGE XX)
6 SCALLIONS, MINCED	¼ CUP COARSE SEMOLINA OR FARINA CEREAL
2 SWEET PLUM TOMATOES, PEELED, SEEDED, AND CHOPPED	SEA SALT AND FRESHLY GROUND BLACK OR WHITE PEPPER
2 TABLESPOONS MINCED FRESH FLAT-LEAF PARSLEY	FRESHLY GRATED PARMIGIANO-REGGIANO OR GRANA PADANO CHEESE, FOR SERVING

1. Warm the olive oil or butter in a medium saucepan. Stir in the scallions and sauté to wilt, about 1 minute. Add the tomatoes and parsley and sauté for an additional minute. Stir in the broth and bring it to a boil. Immediately reduce to a simmer over medium-low heat and whisk in the semolina or farina. Lower the heat to medium-low and simmer, stirring, until the semolina absorbs the liquid thoroughly and the soup coats a wooden spoon—it should be neither too thick nor too thin—about 7 minutes. Take care not to allow the soup to get too dense. Taste and season with salt and pepper.

2. Ladle the soup into serving bowls and sprinkle grated cheese over each portion. Serve at once.

CREAMY TOMATO SOUP

Serves 6 children or 4 adults

I've made this easy and delicious soup for my family and whipped it up for as many as 200 children in no time at all. It was always a big hit at the healthy school lunch program I started at my children's school. Heavy cream gives it silkiness and sheen, but you can make it dairy-free for the lactose-intolerant without any compromise in flavor by substituting coconut milk.

3 TABLESPOONS UNSALTED BUTTER OR EXTRA-VIRGIN OLIVE OIL, OR A COMBINATION

1 ONION, CHOPPED

2½ CUPS CANNED PEELED PLUM TOMATOES IN NATURAL JUICES

10 FRESH BASIL LEAVES

2 SPRIGS FRESH FLAT-LEAF PARSLEY

½ CUP HEAVY CREAM, OR SUBSTITUTE COCONUT MILK

½ TEASPOON SEA SALT, OR TO TASTE

FRESHLY GROUND WHITE PEPPER

1. In a soup kettle, warm the butter or olive oil, or a mixture, if using. Add the onion and sauté over medium heat until the onion is completely soft, about 7 minutes. Stir in the tomatoes and their juices, the basil, and the parsley. Simmer over medium-low heat until the mixture becomes concentrated and aromatic, about 15 minutes. Turn off the heat.

2. Use an immersion blender to puree the tomato mixture until silky. Alternatively, allow the mixture to cool somewhat and puree it in a blender 2 cups at a time, or pass it through a food mill. Return the liquid to the pot and bring to a simmer. Stir in the cream or coconut milk and heat through. Whether using cream or coconut milk, don't allow the soup to boil once it is added; just season with salt and pepper, heat through, and serve.

QUICK GRILLED CHEESE PANINI

Serves 4 children

The differences between American grilled cheese sandwiches and Italian panini lies in the types of fillings and cheeses used. Mozzarella and fontina are typical ingredients because they are, hands down, the best melting cheeses. Children love these panini in particular because they taste like pizza. For the most nutritious version, use whole-grain bread.

8 SLICES WHOLE GRAIN OR WHITE PULLMAN-TYPE BREAD, CRUSTS REMOVED

EXTRA-VIRGIN OLIVE OIL, FOR BRUSHING

½ POUND FRESH MOZZARELLA CUT INTO 8 THIN SLICES ABOUT 1 INCH SMALLER THAN THE BREAD

1 FRESH, VINE-RIPENED TOMATO, CORED AND CUT INTO THIN STRIPS

DRIED OREGANO

SEA SALT

1. Place the slices of bread on a cutting board. Use a pastry brush to spread olive oil lightly over both sides of each slice. Select a skillet large enough to accommodate 8 slices of bread. Alternatively, use a skillet that can accommodate 4 bread slices and make the sandwiches in two batches. Warm the skillet over medium heat for 4 minutes. Place the bread slices in the pan and cook until crisp and light golden brown on one side only, about 3 minutes. Transfer the bread slices to your work surface, crisp side up.

2. Place half of the cheese slices in the center of half the bread slices. Distribute the tomatoes on top, then sprinkle with oregano and salt to taste. Lay the remaining cheese slices over that. Top with the remaining slices of bread, crisp side down, pressing down gently to set.

3. Warm the skillet once again over low heat. Transfer each sandwich in the skillet and place a weight, such as a smaller cast-iron skillet or a plate topped with a heavy can, on top. Cook until crisp and deep golden brown, 2 to 3 minutes per side, then flip the sandwiches back to the first side to reheat and crisp, about 15 seconds. Serve.

ROOT VEGETABLE PUREE
Makes 3 cups

Root vegetables are packed with nutrients and minerals, and babies love their natural sweetness. Use this method to make a creamy baby food of carrots, parsnips, or other vegetables—or a delicious vegetable course for the whole family.

1½ POUNDS FRESH CARROTS OR PARSNIPS	4 TABLESPOONS UNSALTED BUTTER
	4 CUPS WATER, PLUS MORE IF NEEDED

1. Scrape the carrots or parsnips and slice thin.

2. In an ample pot, melt the butter over medium heat. Stir in the carrots or parsnips and the water. Cover and cook until the liquid reduces to about 3 tablespoons and the vegetable is thoroughly softened, about 45 minutes, stirring occasionally. Add a little more water, if necessary, to prevent the puree from drying out.

3. Transfer the carrots or parsnips to a blender or food processor and puree until creamy. Spoon the puree into a food mill or a sieve, pressing to pass the vegetable through the holes. Season as you like with a little more butter or extra-virgin olive oil before serving.

FUSILLI
WITH CREAMY CHEESE SAUCE
Serves 4 children or 2 adults

My children were mad about this simple pasta dish when they were growing up. They begged for it at every meal, and they always wanted to introduce it to every new friend who came for lunch or dinner. It even became standard birthday party fare, by request. The recipe has traveled to more children's households than I can remember, so I offer it here. I use mascarpone, an Italian cream cheese, but it can be made successfully with good-quality American cream cheese.

½ POUND IMPORTED ITALIAN FUSILLI ("CORKSCREW"), RADIATORE ("LITTLE RADIATOR"), OR CONCHIGLIE ("SHELLS"), OR OTHER SHORT CUT PASTA

1 TABLESPOON KOSHER SALT

3 TABLESPOONS UNSALTED BUTTER, SOFTENED

4 OUNCES MASCARPONE OR GOOD-QUALITY CREAM CHEESE, AT ROOM TEMPERATURE

2 TABLESPOONS FRESHLY GRATED PARMIGIANO-REGGIANO OR GRANA PADANO CHEESE

1. Bring 5 quarts water to a boil and stir in the pasta and salt at once. Cook it according to the package directions.

2. Meanwhile, in a double boiler or saucepan over very low heat, melt the butter and stir in the mascarpone or cream cheese, using a whisk to blend. Remove from the heat.

3. Drain the pasta, reserving ¼ cup of the cooking water, and while it is still dripping wet, combine the pasta with the sauce in a serving bowl, tossing to coat the pasta. If necessary, add the reserved cooking water to moisten. Add the grated cheese and toss again. Serve immediately.

PASTINA "STARS"
WITH BUTTER AND MILK

Serves 4 children or 2 adults

Nothing is more emblematic of an Italian childhood that pastina (literally, "little pasta") with butter and milk. It is baby's first solid food, remembered in adulthood with great nostalgia. There are many different varieties of patina, including anellini ("little rings"), stelline ("little stars"), acini de pepe ("peppercorns"), funghetti ("little mushrooms"), alfabeti ("alphabets"), and orzo ("barley"), to name a few of the most common. For best results, save some of the cooking water after draining and add it as needed after stirring in the butter and milk to keep the pastina moist and fluid.

1 CUP "LITTLE STARS" PASTINA OR OTHER TINY PASTINA SHAPES	3 TABLESPOONS UNSALTED BUTTER
3 TEASPOONS SALT	½ CUP WARM MILK, PLUS MORE IF DESIRED

1. Bring 3 quarts water to a boil. Stir in the pastina and salt. Cook according to the package directions. Drain and transfer to a bowl.

2. While still piping hot, add butter to the pasta, burying it in the pasta to melt. Stir in warm milk and serve at once. Add a little more warm milk for a looser texture if desired. Serve immediately to prevent the pastina from drying out and clumping.

TOMATO RICE
WITH MOZZARELLA DICE

Serves 4 to 6 children

This way of cooking rice is called *riso all'Inglese,* "English-style rice," because it is boiled plain, not cooked with a sauce, like a risotto. It was a standby when I was growing up, though it was elaborated on slightly from the original white version with a touch of tomato sauce for color and small pieces of mozzarella. Once folded into the hot rice, the cheese formed long, oozy strands that were fun to eat. If using short-grain rice, follow the method for cooking here; if using a long-grain variety, cook according to the package instructions instead and fold the sauce and cheese in at the end.

1 CUP SHORT-GRAIN RICE SUCH AS ARBORIO, CARNAROLI, OR VIALONE NANO, OR LONG-GRAIN RICE

SEA SALT

½ CUP DICED SMOKED MOZZARELLA OR FRESH MOZZARELLA

2 TABLESPOONS PREPARED TOMATO SAUCE SUCH AS FRUITY NEAPOLITAN TOMATO SAUCE (PAGE 34) OR 20-MINUTE TOMATO SAUCE (PAGE 37), PUREED

1 TABLESPOON UNSALTED BUTTER (OPTIONAL)

1. In a saucepan, bring 3 cups water to a rapid boil. Stir in the rice and a pinch of salt and cover. Cook until done, about 20 minutes.

2. When the rice is cooked, turn off the heat and fold in the cheese, the tomato sauce, and the butter, if using. Serve at once.

12

BASICS

It is a widely accepted notion in Italy that the best cooking is found at home. This is due more to quality and craftsmanship than artistry. The Italian approach is simple. There are a few rudimentary techniques for the application of heat—sautéing, searing, frying, braising, stewing, and roasting, which are described in recipe methods and are easy to follow. A few broths, sauces, basic doughs, and condiments included in this chapter are indispensable. None is elaborate or requires lengthy preparation. The basics described are best homemade because store-bought versions bear little similarity in flavor or goodness. Pre-cooked polenta, solidified and packed in a cellophane tube can be purchased, but it can't compare with what steaming fresh polenta looks like, tastes like, and smells like, or with the way it behaves under a sauce and on the tongue. In short, nothing can replace what good quality does for cooking. Or as the Italians say, "Good with good makes good."

SIGNORA COLUCCIO'S
QUICK LINGUINE AND TOMATO LUNCH

Serves 4 children or 2 adults

Here is a surprising recipe from the Coluccio family, founders of the noteworthy Italian grocery in Brooklyn named Coluccio & Sons—surprising because from a few ordinary ingredients, most of them from the pantry, comes an astonishingly good dish. It is one of those quick dishes that is prepared for hungry children almost instantly and becomes a fond memory of childhood—and a standby in adult life. It works best in small quantities for a pound or less of pasta. Because some of the pasta water serves as a vehicle for the sauce, the dish needs to be eaten immediately while it is still very moist.

8 WHOLE FRESH OR CANNED PEELED PLUM TOMATOES, DRAINED

½ POUND IMPORTED ITALIAN LINGUINE OR SPAGHETTI, BROKEN IN HALF

3 TABLESPOONS KOSHER SALT

6 FRESH BASIL LEAVES, IF AVAILABLE, CHOPPED

4 TABLESPOONS EXTRA-VIRGIN OLIVE OIL

4 TABLESPOONS FRESHLY GRATED PECORINO ROMANO, CACIOCAVALLO, PARMIGIANO-REGGIANO, OR GRANA PADANO CHEESE

1. Bring 2½ quarts water to a rolling boil. Slip in the whole tomatoes and cook for 1 minute. Add the pasta and salt to the water and cook until it is al dente, or according to the directions on the pasta box. Drain the pasta and the tomatoes and reserve about ¼ cup of the pasta cooking water. While the pasta is still dripping wet, transfer it along with the tomatoes to an individual serving dishes.

2. Use a fork to mash up the tomatoes, mixing them with the basil leaves. Add about 1 tablespoon of the reserved pasta water to each serving to moisten the pasta if necessary. Top with the olive oil and cheese and serve at once.

SWEET or SAVORY RICE
COOKED IN MILK

Serves 4 children or 2 adults

Venetian-born Nicoletta Polo is a direct descendant of Marco Polo and takes great pride in her Venetian legacy. She suggested this creamy dish, which Venetian children eat with sugar for breakfast, for an after-school snack, or even for dinner. It is digestible, nourishing, and delicious. You'll need to buy Venetian or other short-grained Italian rice, of which there are three types available: *Vialone Nano* (Veneto rice), *Arborio,* or *Carnaroli.* The family of medium-to-short-grain rices, to which these varieties belong, has the attribute of being able to absorb large quantities of liquid, little by little, without turning to mush. Be sure to add the salt only after cooking to avoid inadvertently oversalting. Savory and sweet versions are included.

1 QUART MILK

1 CUP VIALONE NANO, ARBORIO, OR CARNAROLI SHORT-GRAIN RICE

½ TEASPOON SEA SALT, OR TO TASTE

FOR THE SAVORY VERSION

UNSALTED BUTTER

FRESHLY GRATED PARMIGIANO-REGGIANO CHEESE (OPTIONAL)

FOR THE SWEET VERSION

SUGAR

1. If you are making the savory version, the quantities called for should stand. If you are making the sweet version, however, it should not be as soupy but, instead, *all'onda,* "wavelike," more like a risotto. To achieve this, decrease the milk by about ½ cup, or increase the rice by ¼ cup. If you are making the plain version, neither savory nor sweet, the quantities should also stand.

2. In a saucepan, bring the milk to a gentle boil over medium-low heat. Stir in the rice and salt. Simmer, stirring occasionally, until the rice is soft, about 10 minutes. Season to taste with the butter and cheese, if using, for the savory version or with the sugar for the sweet version, or eat without seasoning.

TASTY MEAT BROTH

Makes 10 cups

Meat broth can provide a delicious starting point for soups. It can also add flavor and moisture to sauces and stews. For maximum flavor, the meat and vegetables should start out cooking in cold water. This way, the meat juices are released into the broth rather than being sealed in by immediate application of intense heat. The best broth is made with a combination of meats.

2 POUNDS CHICKEN BACKS OR WINGS

2 POUNDS BEEF CHUCK, SHANK, OR SHORT RIBS

2 LARGE LEEKS

2 POUNDS VEAL NECK BONES

2 MEDIUM FRESH OR CANNED TOMATOES

2 ONIONS, UNPEELED AND WASHED, QUARTERED

3 LARGE CARROTS, SCRAPED AND CUT INTO QUARTERS

3 LARGE CELERY STALKS, INCLUDING LEAVES

1 BUNCH FLAT-LEAF PARSLEY, STEMS AND LEAVES

1 TEASPOON WHOLE PEPPERCORNS

KOSHER SALT OR SEA SALT

1. Wash the chicken well, removing any excess fat, but keep the skin on. Remove any excess fat from the beef. Trim the root from the leek, slice the leek lengthwise, and spread open the sheaths under the running water to remove any sand. Slice into 1-inch pieces.

2. Select a deep soup kettle into which all the meat will fit comfortably. Add all of the other ingredients except for the salt. Add 10 cups cold water. Cover the pot and bring to a boil. Immediately reduce to medium-low and adjust the heat if necessary to keep the broth at a gentle simmer. Leave the pot partially covered. Skim any foam that forms on the surface. Simmer until full-bodied and tasty, about 4 hours from the boil. The broth should not return to the boil.

3. When the broth is finished, skim off any fat that has risen to the surface. Remove the meat and bones (use the meat for some other purpose). Pass the broth through a fine-mesh sieve. Add salt to taste just before using.

AHEAD-OF-TIME NOTE: This stock can be made up to 4 days in advance. Strain out the meat and vegetables, cover, and refrigerate for up to 4 days, or freeze for up to 3 months. When you are ready to use it, add the salt.

CHICKEN BROTH

Makes 10 cups

Use free-range or organically grown chickens; they have been raised without the antibiotics and other non-food additives of the cage-bred variety and produce a better-tasting broth than do industrially raised chickens. For a rich taste, the proportion of meat to water should be generous.

5 POUNDS CHICKEN WINGS OR BACKS

2 BAY LEAVES

2 MEDIUM ONIONS, UNPEELED AND QUARTERED

2 LARGE CARROTS, SCRAPED AND CUT INTO EIGHT PIECES

2 LARGE CELERY STALKS, INCLUDING LEAVES

2 MEDIUM FRESH OR CANNED TOMATOES

1 SMALL BUNCH FLAT-LEAF PARSLEY, STEMS AND LEAVES

¼ POUND PEELED CELERY ROOT, IF AVAILABLE

2 TEASPOONS WHOLE BLACK OR WHITE PEPPERCORNS

SEA SALT

1. Wash the chicken well, removing any excess fat.

2. Select a deep soup kettle into which the chicken parts will fit comfortably, but not much wider. Put in all of the ingredients except the salt. Add 10 cups cold water. Cover and bring to a boil. Immediately reduce to medium-low and check occasionally, adjusting the heat if necessary to keep the broth at a gentle simmer. Leave the pot partially covered. Skim the surface whenever scum forms. Simmer until the meat falls off the bones, about 90 minutes from the boil.

3. Strain the stock through a fine-mesh sieve. Pick the meat off the bones and reserve for some other purpose. Discard the other solids. Allow the broth to cool at room temperature, then cover and refrigerate for up to 3 days, or freeze for up to 3 months. Add salt to taste just before using.

VEGETABLE BROTH

Makes about 8 cups

Despite their being vegetarians, my children crave the intense flavors of genuine Italian cooking, so I always have rich-tasting vegetable broth on hand as a foundation for soups and other dishes where stock is called for. I have found that sautéeing the vegetables in butter or olive oil prior to cooking produces a tastier broth rather than strictly boiling them.

1 LARGE LEEK, OR 3 BUNCHES SCALLIONS

3 TABLESPOONS UNSALTED BUTTER OR
EXTRA-VIRGIN OLIVE OIL

3 CARROTS, SCRAPED AND SLICED

2 ONIONS, DICED

2 LARGE CELERY STALKS, PLUS THE
LEAVES FROM THE WHOLE CELERY HEAD

2 LARGE BAY LEAVES

8 CUPS WATER

1 TEASPOON BLACK PEPPERCORNS

1 TEASPOON ALLSPICE BERRIES

A HANDFUL OF FLAT-LEAF PARSLEY,
LEAVES AND STEMS

SCANT 1 TABLESPOON SEA SALT,
OR TO TASTE

1. Trim off and discard the roots and discolored parts of the stem of the leek. Slice the leek in half lengthwise and spread open the sheaths under cold running water to wash out any sand that is lodged between them. Slice into 1-inch pieces crosswise.

2. In a large soup kettle over medium-low heat, melt the butter or warm the olive oil. Add the leek, carrots, onion, celery stalks and their leaves, and bay leaves. Sauté the vegetables gently without letting them brown, about 10 minutes. Add 1 cup of the water, stir, and cover. Cook gently for an additional 20 minutes, stirring occasionally.

3. Add the remaining 7 cups water, the peppercorns, allspice, and parsley. Cover and cook over low heat for 1½ hours. Strain through a fine-mesh strainer. Season with the salt.

AHEAD-OF-TIME NOTE: This broth can be made 2 or 3 days in advance of using, cooled, covered, and refrigerated. Or it can be frozen for up to 3 months.

RAPHAEL BOERI'S
MILK DOUGH for YEAST BREAD
For 1 focaccia, 2 pizzas, or 2 breads

Raphael Boeri is a French pastry chef who spent many years working in Italy learning the breadmaker's art. His yeast dough, learned from a Milanese baker and *pizzaiolo*, incorporates milk and egg, resulting in a tender, richly flavored crust with a crispy skin. When I first ate it in a rustic *pissaladella* (page 22) that Raphael created for the Didier Dumas Patisserie in my village, it was a revelation to me. You can use it for any pizza, focaccia, or yeast bread base, whether baked or fried—or for loaf bread. Note that a tablespoon and a half of beaten egg is called for, as measurements need to be precise. You can easily double the recipe, using a total of one large egg to make measuring easier. Then divide the dough in half and freeze the portion you don't use immediately. For the experienced baker, who always prefers precise metric measures, I include both American and metric measurements.

1 CUP/200G OR MORE WARM WATER

2 7-OUNCE PACKAGES ACTIVE DRY YEAST/15G FRESH BAKER'S YEAST

⅓ CUP/12ML EXTRA-VIRGIN OLIVE OIL

1½ TABLESPOONS/15G BEATEN EGG

⅛ CUP/25ML MILK, AT ROOM TEMPERATURE

4 CUPS/500G UNBLEACHED ALL-PURPOSE FLOUR

2 TEASPOONS/12G SEA SALT

PINCH/ 2G SUGAR

1. Place ¼ cup (130g) warm water in a medium bowl. Stir in the yeast. Let the mixture stand in a warm place until it becomes foamy, about 10 minutes.

2. In another bowl, combine the remaining ¾ cup warm water, the olive oil, beaten egg, and milk.

3. In the bowl of an electric stand mixer fitted with a dough hook, combine the flour, salt, and sugar. Turn the mixer on low and mix until the dough is smooth and somewhat sticky, 6 to 7 minutes, stopping occasionally to scrape down the sides and base of the bowl. Add 1 to 2 teaspoons more warm water as necessary to make a dough that is cohesive and smooth, but still lightly sticky to the touch.

4. Place the dough in a lightly oiled bowl. Lightly brush the dough with some oil. Cover completely with dampened clean kitchen towels. Allow to rise at room temperature in a draft-free location until doubled, about 45 minutes. The dough can now be formed into *pissaladella* (page 22), pizza, calzone (page 20), or loaves. For *pissaladella* or calzone, the dough does not need to rise again. For bread, form the dough into braided or rounded loaves, cover with dampened towels, and let rise until doubled. Preheat an oven to 400°F and bake until done, about 20 minutes.

BASIC POLENTA

Serves 6

Probably few things are more reminiscent of Italian home cooking than polenta, which is nothing more than a cornmeal porridge. In its simplest guise, it is served in that form with butter and a hard grating cheese, or with a soft, runny cheese (see Steaming Polenta with Taleggio Cheese, page 106). Or it can be topped with a meat or mushroom sauce or a stew; a particularly happy union is polenta with Viola Buitoni's Long-Simmered Tomato Sauce with Ribs and Sausages (page 42). Polenta can also be turned out onto a marble slab or another hard surface, allowed to become firm, then cut into squares. These pieces have endless uses, especially for antipasti. Whether fried or sautéed in olive oil, or brushed with olive oil and grilled, they become *crostini di polenta,* delicious crunchy "toasts." Note that polenta must be made from polenta cornmeal. Cooked ground corn used for corn bread will not result in an edible cornmeal porridge.

7 CUPS WATER	2 CUPS POLENTA CORNMEAL
1 TABLESPOON KOSHER SALT	BOILING WATER, AS NEEDED

1. Bring the water to a boil in a deep pot. Add the salt and bring the heat down to medium. Then add the cornmeal very slowly, almost in a trickle (*a doccia,* "like a shower"); this gradual introduction of cornmeal to the boiling water prevents lumps from forming. Keep the polenta at a constant simmer and, from the instant the cornmeal is added to the water, continuously stir it with a long-handled wooden spoon or whisk, always in the same direction. After all the cornmeal is absorbed, continue to stir until the polenta is thick and pulls away easily from the sides of the pan. If the polenta is quite thick but still not pulling, add a little more boiling water and continue to stir until it is ready. It should be perfectly cooked, thick, and creamy in 25 to 30 minutes.

2. If serving loose, pour into a platter at once, dress according to your recipe, and serve. For polenta crostini, pour the hot polenta out onto a clean oiled work surface and use a rubber spatula to spread to a thickness of ¼ inch. Allow it to set and grill or fry, as preferred.

HOMEMADE MAYONNAISE
WITH VARIATIONS

Makes 1 cup

There is no equal to homemade mayonnaise, and it is very easy to prepare with a blender. It is important that your utensils be warm and that all the ingredients be at room temperature, that is, out of the refrigerator for an hour or more. While classic recipes for mayonnaise call for two egg yolks, for this quantity of oil, I like to use a whole egg instead. It makes the mayonnaise lighter and more nutritious (egg white is pure protein). Use this light, silky dressing (see variations below) on freshly boiled meat or vegetables, steamed lobster, or warm boiled potatoes, just to name a few possibilities.

½ CUP GRAPE SEED OIL OR OTHER VEGETABLE OIL

¼ CUP EXTRA-VIRGIN OLIVE OIL

1 LARGE EGG, AT ROOM TEMPERATURE

½ TEASPOON SALT, OR TO TASTE

2 TABLESPOONS FRESHLY SQUEEZED LEMON JUICE, OR TO TASTE

1 TEASPOON DIJON MUSTARD

DASH OF FRESHLY GROUND WHITE PEPPER

Combine the oils in a small pitcher. Crack the egg into the blender and pulse for 3 seconds. Add 2 tablespoons of the oils. Blend on high speed for 10 seconds. With the machine running, add the remaining oil in a very thin, slow, steady stream. Turn off the blender and use a rubber spatula to scrape the inside so that all the ingredients are thoroughly combined. Stir the salt into the lemon juice and add it with the mustard and pepper. Blend to combine thoroughly. Use immediately, or cover and chill. Homemade mayonnaise will keep for a week in the refrigerator.

NOTE: If the mayonnaise separates, bring it and an egg to room temperature. Break the yolk into a mixing bowl and whisk in the broken mayonnaise by tablespoon until the mixture is cohesive, then add in a bit of whichever oil you used to set the mayonnaise.

FOR GARLIC MAYONNAISE: Mince 3 large cloves garlic, then pound into a paste with a little salt and a pinch of cayenne pepper. Blend with 1 cup mayonnaise.

FOR LIGHT LEMON MAYONNAISE: Blend the mayonnaise with additional freshly squeezed lemon juice to taste. Thin with a little water until the mayonnaise reaches a pourable but still very creamy consistency.

FOR HORSERADISH MAYONNAISE: To 1 cup mayonnaise, blend a 2-inch piece of fresh horseradish root, grated, or ¼ cup prepared white horseradish, or to taste, and 2 tablespoons Dijon mustard.

NEW WORLD
FLAKY PASTRY DOUGH

Makes 2 crusts or 16 tartlets

I call this "New World" pastry dough because flaky pie crusts, which I love, are an English and American invention. When it comes to fruit pies, I much prefer them to the *pasta frolla*-type pastry crust of the Italians. This exceptional pie crust recipe was developed by my friend, food writer and pastry expert Susan G. Purdy. It is buttery in flavor, flaky in texture, and incredibly easy to handle. This dough is most quickly prepared in a food processor fitted with a steel blade. For best results, use a combination of frozen butter and well-chilled or frozen non-transfat vegetable shortening (measure onto wax paper and freeze about 30 minutes before starting). For dessert pies, add sugar and one large egg yolk as part of the measured liquid. For savory meat fillings, omit the sugar and add one whole large egg.

3 CUPS ALL-PURPOSE FLOUR

¾ TEASPOON SALT

OPTIONAL SWEETENER FOR DESSERT PIES: 1½ TO 2 TABLESPOONS SUGAR

12 TABLESPOONS UNSALTED BUTTER, WELL CHILLED OR FROZEN, CUT UP

6 TABLESPOONS TRANS-FAT-FREE SOLID VEGETABLE SHORTENING SUCH AS CRISCO, OR LARD, CHILLED OR FROZEN

1 LARGE EGG (OR ONE LARGE YOLK, SEE NOTE ABOVE)

1 TABLESPOON LEMON JUICE OR UNFLAVORED VINEGAR

3 TO 5 TABLESPOONS ICE WATER, JUST AS NEEDED

EGG GLAZE (OPTIONAL)

1 WHOLE EGG BEATEN WITH 1 TEASPOON WATER

1. TO PREPARE PASTRY IN A FOOD PROCESSOR: Combine flour, salt, and sugar if used; pulse a few times to blend. Add the butter and solid vegetable shortening and pulse only until fat is cut into bits the size of peas. Through the feed tube, add the egg and lemon juice or vinegar, pulse once or twice, then add ice water one tablespoon at a time, pulsing once or twice between additions, only until the dough begins to show some clumps. Do not form a dough ball on the blade.

2. Turn the dough out onto a piece of wax paper (if it looks sandy and dry, sprinkle on a tiny bit more water) and use your hands to bring it together into a ball; the dough should hold the form of your fingers when squeezed. Wrap up the dough and refrigerate for at least 30 minutes. To use, roll out on a lightly floured surface with a floured rolling pin. Note: If the butter and vegetable shortening were frozen, the dough can be rolled without prior chilling.

OPTIONAL: To give a golden finish to the tops of formed pies or tartlets, use a pastry brush to coat them with the egg glaze just before baking.

INDEX

ACKNOWLEDGMENTS

I am grateful to Anja Schmidt and to Kyle Cathie for the opportunity to write this book and to Carole Bidnick for shepherding it beyond what could be expected from any literary agent. And I thank my writing colleague, Bill Marsano, for his enthusiast support for this project at the outset and for his generous help with advice, information, and writing.

It all began with a fine pile of hand-written recipes from my aunt and gifted cook, Rita Ghisu, who has comforted so many with her generous hospitality and remarkably good food; she is precisely the kind of cook to whom this book pays homage. So is Anna Amendolara Nurse, who besides offering her Pugliese recipes, which I love so much, has been a tireless mentor for over two decades, illuminating my professional path. For many comforting meals and for generously sharing her hand-written heirloom recipes, I am indebted to Anna Maria Weld.

Only my *amica stretta* and fellow author, Susan G. Purdy, knows the joys and torments of crafting a cookbook that you hope will convey what you want to say; I am so grateful for her advice.

I would also like to thank Nick Malgieri, Viola Buitoni, Donatella Platoni, Cathy Coluccio, Nicoletta Polo Lanza Tomasi, duchess of Palma, Baron Giuseppe Rosso, Rena Glickman, Nick Gualano, Didier Duma and Raphael Boeri for research on my behalf and permission to reproduce their recipes; also to Sophie Giovanola, Lorraine Petrucci, Anna Palaia, Gina Quatrocchi, Francesco Fiondello, and Olimpia Fiondello for sharing family

recipes and for their efforts on my behalf; and to Mary Wallace, Joan Gussow, Barbara Bedway, and Greg Mitchell for tasting works in progress. Thanks are due also to Augusto Marchini and the Italian Trade Commission, Gruppo Ristoratori Italiani, and Oldways Preservation Trust for all I have learned during so many travels in Italy at their invitation. I am especially grateful to Flavia Destefanis for such generous research and Italian editing on yet another of my books; Laurel Robertson for months of recipe testing and help with field work; and Elizabeth Walber for working with me in the kindest and most generous way doing many hours of editing.

Perhaps the most thanks should go to the many Italian people whose names I never knew or cannot remember, who have offered their food and recipes with such generosity.

Having a visual bent, I believe that what makes a cookbook come alive besides its honesty are illustrations that can draw the reader in as few words alone can do. I am delighted with the exquisite photographs for this book that were taken by Christopher Hirsheimer and Melissa Hamilton, and that so perfectly express the simple goodness and timeless appeal of Italian home cooking.

Above all, I thank my good and beautiful children, Gabriella and Celina della Croce, for their constant support and enthusiasm for my cooking; Katie and Charlie Hoyt for their graceful presence at the new family table even if the food is sometimes exotic to them; and my husband Nathan Hoyt, who is an inexhaustible source of inspiration.